The Role of the third Surveyor

under the Party Wall etc. Act 1996

Victor H Vegoda FRICS IRRV FBEng MEWI

A division of Reed Business Information

Estates Gazette
1 Procter Street, London WC1V 6EU

ISBN 0 7282 0462 2

Copies of Acts of Parliament and parts thereof reproduced by the kind permission of Her Majesty's Stationery Office

Typeset in Palatino by Amy Boyle, Rochester, Kent
Printed by Bell & Bain Ltd., Glasgow

Contents

Table of Cases

Table of Statutes

The beginning

In the beginning, there was a notice and it was good. If it had not been good, the notice would have been invalid and everything that followed would have been of no effect.[1]

The notice should be accompanied by a friendly letter clearly explaining the procedure: and a personal visit, if appropriate, will often smooth the way.

Notices

The notice will either be under:

- s 1 of the Act – Line of junction notice
- s 2 of the Act – A party structure notice
- s 6 of the Act – A three metre or a six metre notice.

---

[1] *Gyle-Thompson* v *Wall Street (Properties) Ltd* [1974] 1 All ER 295. A notice and an award were sent to a surveyor who had been advising but had not been authorised to accept service of either. In fact, the surveyor had never been formally appointed as a party wall surveyor. Both the notice and the award were therefore ineffective because of the lack of appointment and for the reason that the 1939 Act did not authorise the reduction in height of a wall. The surveyors therefore exceeded their powers in authorising it. This is why it is now customary for surveyors to request a copy of the other surveyor's letter of appointment.

Adjoining owner's options

- Agree to the works. Such agreement must be in writing in accordance with s 3(3) of the Act.
- Both parties to appoint an "agreed surveyor" in accordance with s 10(1)(a). He will act in the interests of both parties and will ultimately serve an award or awards upon the parties.
- Each party to appoint a surveyor in accordance with s 10(1)(b).

It is only under the third option that a third surveyor can be selected and if necessary, appointed.

Surveyors appointments and selection

The only part of the Act which makes mention of third surveyors is s 10 of the Act. I will take you through it.

> 10(1)(b) each party shall appoint a surveyor and the two surveyors so appointed shall forthwith select a third surveyor (all of whom are in this section referred to as "the three surveyors").

It is important that the third surveyor is selected "forthwith", because once a dispute arises which the two surveyors are unable to resolve, they may not be able to agree anything, let alone the selection of someone to resolve their disputes.

Appointments under the Act are personal appointments and are irrevocable except in special circumstances.

> 10(5) If, before the dispute is settled, a surveyor appointed under paragraph (b) of subsection (1) by a party to the dispute dies, or becomes or deems himself incapable of acting, the party who appointed him may appoint another surveyor in his place with the same power and authority.

Whether a surveyor becomes incapable of acting or just stubbornly refuses to act, as has happened in my experience is a grey area. You will see therefore that it is not easy to divest oneself of a surveyor once appointed. Recourse by the aggrieved party to the third surveyor may circumvent the problem.

Firms or companies cannot be appointed. In large practices, this is often resolved by a partner being appointed and delegating the work to an assistant. If the assistant leaves, he will not then take the instruction and the fee attached to it, with him.

If the two surveyors are unable to agree upon a third surveyor, the procedure in s 10(8) of the Act may be invoked.

> If either surveyor appointed under subsection (1)(b) by a party to the dispute refuses to select a third surveyor under subsection (1) or (9), or neglects to do so for a period of ten days beginning with the day on which the other surveyor serves a request on him –
>
> (a)   the appointing officer; or
> (b)   in cases where the relevant appointing officer or his employer is a Party to the dispute, the Secretary of State, may on the application of either surveyor select a third surveyor who shall have the same power and authority as if he had been selected under subsection (1) or subsection (9).

The selected surveyor does not have to accept the appointment. If he dithers, dies or cannot cope, the two surveyors must start again.

> (9) If a third surveyor selected under subsection (1)(b) –
>
> (a)   refuses to act;
> (b)   neglects to act for a period of ten days beginning with the day on which either party or the surveyor appointed by either party serves a request on him; or
> (c)   dies, or becomes or deems himself incapable of acting, before the dispute is settled,
>
> the other two of the three surveyors shall forthwith select another surveyor in his place with the same power and authority.

The building owner, the adjoining owner and one or both of the surveyors can call upon the third surveyor to resolve their disputes.

> 10(11) Either of the parties or either of the surveyors appointed by the parties may call upon the third surveyor selected in pursuance of this section to determine the disputed matters and he shall make the necessary award.

The surveyors and the third surveyor can only award on the subject-matter of the notice. They do not have the power under the Act to resolve other disputes, though there is nothing to prevent the parties from agreeing outside the Act to abide by a decision of one or more of the surveyors.[2]

---

2   *Woodhouse* v *Consolidated Property Corporation Ltd* [1993] EGLR 174, CA.

10(12) An award may determine –

(a) the right to execute any work;

(b) the time and manner of executing any work; and

(c) any other matter arising out of or incidental to the dispute including the costs of making the award;

but any period appointed by the award for executing any work shall not unless otherwise agreed between the building owner and the adjoining owner begin to run until after the expiration of the period prescribed by this Act for service of the notice in respect of which the dispute arises or is deemed to have arisen.

Third surveyor awards, unlike those of the surveyors appointed by the parties, do not have to be served "forthwith": see s 10(14). He awards his own fees and need not serve the award until he is paid.

10(15) Where an award is made by the third surveyor—

(a) he shall, after payment of the costs of the award, serve it forthwith on the parties or their appointed surveyors; and

(b) if it is served on their appointed surveyors, they shall serve it forthwith on the parties.

My own practise is to serve the third surveyor's award, both on the parties and the appointed surveyors.

Who can be a party wall surveyor or a third surveyor?

Anyone other than a party to the dispute. That is anyone except the building owner or the adjoining owner: see s 20.

"surveyor" means any person not being a party to the matter appointed or selected under section 10 to determine disputes in accordance with the procedures set out in this Act.

I once agreed to be appointed as a party wall surveyor by very old friends. The husband was a *de facto* director of the company but he was not on the board and his wife owned all the shares. Things went well and awards were signed and served. However, towards the end of the development my friend interfered to such an extent that I deemed myself incapable of acting and withdrew. I suggested, tongue in cheek, that as the property was owned by his wife's company, she could appoint him to act as party wall surveyor in my place.

How do you choose a third surveyor?

Usually, the surveyor appointed by the building owner[1] will write to the surveyor appointed by the adjoining owner suggesting three names for selection as third surveyor.[2] Usually the adjoining owner's surveyor will accept one or other of the names suggested. This will be recorded by both surveyors and will subsequently appear in the award.

The adjoining owner's surveyor does not necessary have to accept one of the surveyors suggested by the building owner's surveyor. He can come back with his own suggestions. I often do when confronted with a list of surveyors from large and expensive practices which are not particularly close to the site of the subject property.

Choosing a third surveyor is difficult if you do not know anything about the person, as is often the case. I generally accept members of the

---

[1] The surveyor appointed by the building owner, (the person doing the development) is usually referred to as the building owner's surveyor. This is often abbreviated to BOS. The surveyor appointed by the adjoining owner is generally called the adjoining owner's surveyor. (AOS). The building owner and the adjoining owner are abbreviated BO and AO. The third surveyor who is selected by the two appointed surveyors is abbreviated to TS. In fact all the three surveyors are supposed to be independent regardless of who appointed them, though the appointed surveyors may have regard to the interest of the person who appointed them.

[2] This is just custom. It is not a matter of law.

Pyramus and Thisbe Club.[3] This is a club for party wall surveyors. Members can be expected to have some knowledge of the Act but it is not always the case that they do.

The Royal Institution of Chartered Surveyors also has a list of party wall surveyors and there is a new organisation called the Faculty of Party Wall Surveyors about which I have no knowledge other than the name.

The selected surveyor does not have to be told and if all goes smoothly, may never be aware that he has been selected. If approached to act, he does not have to accept the appointment and may deem himself incapable of acting: see s 10(9). A new selection will then have to be agreed.

A selection is not an appointment. Appointment only arises if the two surveyors are unable to agree and one or both refer the matter to the third surveyor and he agrees to accept the appointment.

---

[3]   A club for party wall surveyors. It was formed by the late John Anstey to encourage knowledge about party walls and is named after the lovers in A Mid Summer Night's Dream, who met through a chink in the wall.

What are the third surveyor duties?

- To resolve disputes which are placed before him[1] as third surveyor.
  He will award on the matter in dispute. He will award his own fees and decide who pays them and he can await payment before serving the award on the surveyors or the parties: see s 10(15). I generally serve it on both the parties and the surveyors. If the notice is served on the surveyors only, they must forthwith serve it on the parties.
- Join with one or both of the two surveyors appointed by the parties, if requested to do so, in making an award under the Act unless he deems a third surveyor's award more appropriate.
  The surveyors making the award will then forthwith serve the award upon the appointing owners.
- Guide either or both of the surveyors if they seek advice from him during the course of a dispute.

Where this occurs, it is not usual for the third surveyor to make any charge unless he does more than speak on the telephone.

Members of the Pyramus and Thisbe Club deem it their duty to spread understanding of the Act whether they are appointed in the matter or are just helping a perplexed fellow party wall surveyor with advice.

---

[1] Him or her. Please take as read that the feminine may be substituted for the masculine.

My experience of good third surveyors is that they can, by their guidance, help to achieve agreement. In one case, I was appointed by the building owner who was at odds with his neighbour before the party wall procedure started. My appointing owner wished to erect an independent wall on the line of junction which, by itself would not have met the requirements of building regulations. However, because the neighbouring wall was present, it complied. We awarded that both walls were independent wholly owned walls and were therefore not capable of being the subject of an award. We awarded on other matters relating to changes in a soil retaining wall and ground slab which abutted the adjacent wall and on the weathering. The guidance of the third surveyor was key to the agreement and he made no award and no charge.

The third surveyor should not introduce new complications to exacerbate the dispute. On the contrary, he should try to simplify and reduce the issues in dispute with a view to assisting an agreement between the two surveyors.

If he cannot achieve an agreement, he should take representations from each surveyor; allow each surveyor to comment upon the other surveyor's representations and as quickly as possible, he should award to resolve the dispute.

He should promptly return telephone calls and reply to letters and exert himself to bring harmony where there is discord.

Once he has awarded, the parties, but not the surveyors, have 14 days beginning on the day which they receive it, to appeal the award: see s 10(17).

> Either of the parties to the dispute may, within the period of fourteen days beginning with the day on which an award made under this section is served on him, appeal to the county court against the award and the county court may –
>
> (a) rescind the award or modify it in such manner as the court thinks fit; and
>
> (b) make such order as to costs as the court thinks fit.

"Surveyor" is defined in s 20 of the Act as follows:

> "surveyor" means any person not being a party to the matter appointed or selected under section 10 to determine disputes in accordance with the procedures set out in this Act.

Section 10(17) says "parties" not "surveyors" and as s 20 makes clear a surveyor cannot be a party, a surveyor cannot appeal.

It says much for the effectiveness of the system that I was only able to find four reported cases relating to third surveyors. Two of the cases only made a passing reference to a third surveyor and the other two are relevant and are reproduced in full in this book. Neither of the cases are under the current Act. They were dealt with during the currency of the London Building Acts (Amendment) Act 1939.

Who may apply to the third surveyor? How to do it

One or more of the parties and/or the surveyors may apply to the third surveyor if they have a dispute which they are unable to resolve.
Section 10(11) says:

> 10(11) Either of the parties or either of the surveyors appointed by the parties may call upon the third surveyor selected in pursuance of this section to determine the disputed matters and he shall make the necessary award.

Most such applications are made by surveyors. Surveyors contemplating an application should bear in mind that the third surveyor will award his own fees against one or more of the parties. They should therefore advise their appointing owner of the risk. Applications should not be made frivolously and appointing owners should be made aware, before an application is made by a surveyor, that they stand at risk of having to pay the third surveyor's fees or a proportion of them.

A party may be dissatisfied with their own appointed surveyor and make a third surveyor application as a means of resolving an otherwise difficult state of affairs.

Where an application is made, it is best for those applying to agree the matters in dispute so that the third surveyor clearly understands the points at issue. This is not always possible. Occasions do arise where surveyors behave unprofessionally and lack the detachment required of them. This can also happen to appointing owners. Where possible, a joint or agreed letter to the third surveyor will help to clarify points which might otherwise emerge only slowly and painfully.

One advantage of the third surveyor system of resolving disputes is that it is usually inexpensive as compared with other methods of resolving disputes.

Once a third surveyor award has been served, the parties still have 14 days including the date of service to appeal it to a county court should they wish to do so.[1] Appealing an award through the court is potentially very expensive and not to be undertaken lightly.

---

[1]   s 10(17).

What should the third surveyor do?

Accept the appointment. If he rules himself incapable of acting, he will not be third surveyor and the selection of third surveyor will have to start anew.[1]

If there is a full blown dispute which has been placed before the third surveyor and it has not been possible for it to be compromised, the third surveyor will immediately want to have copies of:

- letters of appointment of the surveyors to ensure the Act has been complied with. All appointments must be in writing[2]
- notices served[3]
- the award (if any)
- any relevant correspondence.

These should be provided with the letter addressed to the third surveyor setting out the basis of the dispute and requesting him to deal with it. A copy of the letter should be sent to the other surveyor and to the parties because ultimately, one of them will be picking up the bill.

---

[1] Party Wall etc. Act 1996 s 10(9).
[2] Party Wall etc. Act 1996 s 10(2).
[3] Party Wall etc. Act 1996.
    s 3 notice for work in s 2
    s 4 – counter notice
    s 6 – 3 m or 6 m notices
    s 15 – rules for service.

The third surveyor may need to visit the site. If there are technical matters outside his area of competence, at issue, he must take advice from someone who is competent in that field. The cost of this advice will be included in the award.

Before taking any action and racking up fees, the third surveyor should encourage the parties to the dispute to reach an agreement without him.

Above all, nothing should be done which is not transparent. All correspondence and/or communications with the third surveyor should be disclosed to the other appointed surveyor. Should that not be the case, the third surveyor may be accused of partiality or bias and any award that he makes may be open to challenge. In such a case, it may be that a court would waive the 14-day limit imposed by s 10(17) of the Act because of the patent unfairness of the procedure. I have seen correspondence where a third surveyor threatened to award on undisclosed matters, with the adjoining owner's surveyor, though no approach had been made to the other appointed surveyor concerning the subject-matter of the proposed award. Such behaviour strikes at the very spirit of the Act and I believe it would bring opprobrium on those acting in this unjust manner.[4]

When awarding, he should clearly set out:

- the names and addresses of the parties
- the names and addresses of their surveyors
- the addresses of the properties involved
- the date of the notice and the sections of the Act under which it was served
- details of his own appointment
- the nature of the dispute
- his findings and award
- some surveyors prefer a reasoned award and others do not. It has been said that a reasoned award will usually give the right decision and the wrong reason
- the award should be signed and dated.

The Act does not require any Award to be witnessed. The custom has grown up that surveyors have one witness to their signature unless they

---

4   See *Amec Capital Projects Ltd* v *Whitefriars City Estates Ltd* [2004] EWCA Civ 1418.

sign the award in each other's presence. It is therefore a matter for the third surveyor, whether or not he decides to have his award witnessed.

Having made his award he has a duty to serve it:

10(15) Where an award is made by the third surveyor –

   (a)   he shall, after payment of the costs of the award, serve it forthwith on the parties or their appointed surveyors; and

   (b)   if it is served on their appointed surveyors, they shall serve it forthwith on the parties.

Having laid the groundwork, I am going to regale you with some third surveyor stories relating to cases in which I played a part.

The case of the missing surveyor

This matter related to adjoining mid terrace houses in an inner London borough. The building owner wanted to underpin a party wall, shared with my appointing owners.

I was opposed to underpinning because the damage was minor and did not warrant it. Heaven knows how insurers were persuaded to meet the cost of the works. I am opposed to underpinning parts only of terraces. It creates a fixed point and sets up strains which lead to cracking and distortion in other parts of the terrace.

I and the building owner's surveyor; an engineer, could not agree an award. He wanted my appointing owners to pay half the cost of underpinning the party wall citing s 11 of the Act. Neither I nor my appointing owners wanted it underpinned at all. Paying for the unwanted work would have added insult to injury. My argument was that as there was no significant damage on my appointing owners' side of the wall, no contribution was required.

The building owner had a right to underpin and so we agreed a schedule of condition. Disputed matters were to be referred to the third surveyor. We signed and served an award on that basis.

The building owner's surveyor then disappeared from view and the third surveyor, a member of the Pyramus and Thisbe Club, was appointed and wrote lengthy letters which instead of reducing the matters in contention attempted to introduce further matters. These would have made the dispute even more intractable.

Furthermore, the third surveyor refused to inspect the properties unless the building owner's surveyor was also present but he had gone to ground and did not return telephone calls or respond to letters. I could see no way out of this impasse.

After nearly three months without progress, I served a 10-day letter under s 10(6) on the building owner's surveyor at his last known address. He had moved without telling me his new address though none of my letters were returned. I sent a copy to the third surveyor.

Section 10 (6) says:

If a surveyor –

(a) appointed under paragraph (b) of subsection (1) by a party to the dispute; or

(b) appointed under subsection (4) or (5),

refuses to act effectively, the surveyor of the other party may proceed to act *ex parte* and anything so done by him shall be as effectual as if he had been an agreed surveyor.

With hindsight I realise that I should also have served a s 10(6) notice on the third surveyor because he was also appointed under s 10(1)(b).

I managed to speak to the appointing owner's surveyor some days after having served the s 10(6) notice and he promised to deal with the matter within days but failed to do so. I therefore, served an *ex parte* award following which things happened very quickly.

An 11th hour appeal was mounted against the award. To this day I do not believe that the building owner's surveyor had instructions to appeal and as a surveyor he could not himself appeal. Only a party can appeal[1] and a surveyor cannot be a party.[2]

In the meantime, I was trying to resolve matters through the loss adjusters. The adjoining owner's loss adjuster proved to be a broken reed, but eventually I was able to contact the building owner's loss adjuster. He was a gentleman and was a willing party in assisting to resolve the dispute. We had a round table meeting at his office. He and a senior colleague and we two surveyors were present and hammered out an agreement we could all live with.

However, the building owner's surveyor, whose agreement had been reluctant, effectively sabotaged our agreement. I believe that he felt the matter personally and his judgment was clouded. His pursuit

---

[1] See s 10(17).

[2] See s 20.

of the appeal ran up the most enormous fees which were ultimately paid by the building owner's insurers.

There were two expensive hearings before the appeal was withdrawn.

I believe that the reason for withdrawal, was the inability of the appointing owner's surveyor to produce written instructions from his appointing owner, to bring an appeal.

The epilogue is that structural movement continued to take place in the adjoining owner's property and their insurers accepted the claim.

I would not be surprised to learn that the damage is continuing along the terrace, where it will end when it reaches the flank wall.

I doubt whether the building owner's surveyor received any fees and I am told that he had to pay the legal fees personally.

The case of the aloof third surveyor

I was approached via e-mail by a gentleman in Canada who found me on the internet and wanted me to deal with a party wall notice on behalf of his elderly sister. The proposed works were an attic extension to form a room or rooms in the neighbouring roof space.

Before I became involved, there was already bad blood between the two owners: the result of some damage to the adjoining owner's fence caused by the building owner's workmen, which had never been paid for.

The roof extension was to be carried out under permitted development and would extend to half the thickness of the party wall. I objected to this because it would prejudice my appointing owner, should she or her successors wish to develop in the same way in the future.

The building owner's surveyor was an elderly gentleman and a chartered engineer. He knew he was right and nothing would move him. He wrote long rambling letters quoting from Part VI of the London Building Acts (Amendment) Act 1939. This had never applied in the outer London boroughs and has been superseded by the Party Wall etc. Act 1996. Being certain of my ground I was equally implacable and so we were not going to reach an agreement.

The only thing we could agree on was the name of the third surveyor. He had put forward one name and he happened to be a member of the Pyramus and Thisbe Club. I spoke to him on the telephone and he seemed to be reasonable, so I accepted him.

About a ream of paper later, I made an approach to the third surveyor to try to resolve the matter. In fact I made a number of approaches and I didn't get any replies to my letters and telephone calls were not returned.

When I did get to speak on the telephone, promises to deal with the matter were not kept – probably due to inexperience.

This was not a case where I thought an *ex parte* award would be appropriate.

For one thing I couldn't claim that the building owner's surveyor had failed to act effectively.[1] Every time I wrote a letter he responded with aggressive and libellous replies.

There were two matters at issue here. One was whether the building owner had a right to build up only over half the party wall.[2] I have to tell you that opinions among surveyors, who are members of the Party

---

[1] *Frances Holland School* v *Wassef* [2001] Central London County Court.

[2] The reason the building owners wished to insert their wall was because they believed that under the rules for permitted development, they could only build to the extent of their boundary, which was shown on the title documents as being the centre line of the party wall on each side. Since this dispute was settled, I have learned of a decision which allows permitted development to the full extent of the party wall. It was a decision by RO Evans a planning inspector, dated 11 October 2001. Reference APP/Q5300/X/01/1062324 against a refusal by the London Borough of Enfield of an application of Mr N Brade for a certificate of lawful development for an L-shaped roof extension because it was for the full width of the party wall and therefore outside the cartilage of the development.

In his decision, the inspector said, *inter alia*:

"**Conclusion**

9. In terms of its functional relationship to the building and the area it occupies, I conclude that the party wall falls within the curtilage of the dwellinghouse for the purposes of the GPDO, even if that might not be so, for example, in conveyancing terms. It follows that to extend it in the manner specified would fall within the GPDO provisions. I have considered all other matters raised, but in the absence of any considered all other matters raised, but in the absence of any other objection, none serves to overturn this conclusion and the appeal should thus be allowed.

Formal Decision

In exercise of the powers transferred to me, I allow the appeal and I attach to this decision a certificate of lawfulness describing the proposed operation which I consider to be lawful."

Wall & Rights to Light Forum,[3] are sharply divided but I am firmly on the side of those who believe that it should not or cannot be done because it prejudices the adjoining owner's rights in the future.

If the extension was inset away from the party wall, then the only reason a party wall notice had to be served was to insert steels into the party wall.

The building owner needed access to the adjoining land in order to erect a scaffold to access the cheeks of the dormer. If the dormer window was inset, there was no right of access under the Party Wall etc. Act 1996 because the work to the dormer would not then be "work in pursuance of the Act"[4] because no notice would have had to have been served for it to be done. I think there is a general consensus among party wall surveyors that any work for which a notice has to be served under the Act is "work in pursuance of the Act".

Whether the work, for which notices do not have to be served, is work in pursuance of the Act is open to debate but I would doubt it. The right of access is only for work in pursuance of the Act.

Ultimately, I decided that if I could not reach an agreement with the building owner's surveyor and I could not get a meaningful response from the third surveyor, the only way forward was to see if we could reach an agreement under s 3(3) of the Act. That is an informal agreement in writing.

I asked the building owners to come to see me and I could see from their demeanour why the neighbours had fallen out. Word of this meeting must have got back to the third surveyor. I think that the building owners telephoned him directly. Whatever the cause, he was galvanised into life and suddenly there was communication and we agreed a joint award and served it.

This left the original surveyor out in the cold. The award inset the dormer window so that it was not work in pursuance of the Act, which meant that the building owners could not as of right erect a scaffold on the adjoining owner's land.

I persuaded my appointing owner to grant a licence and set out stringent terms.

Because of the bad blood between the parties, I had already served notice under s 12(1) and arranged for a security of £2000 to be deposited with a solicitor nominated by the building owner. Notice

---

3   partywalls@jiscmail.ac.uk.
4   See s 8.

under this section must be given before the commencement of the work.

Because the work of erecting the scaffold on my appointing owner's land was work outside the Act, I inserted conditions in the licence that the security also applied to this work and that in the event of a dispute which could not be resolved between the parties, it would be referred to the small claims section of the county court.

Work was concluded without incident and the deposit returned.

Lessons from the reported third surveyor cases

Chartered Society of Physiotherapy v *Simmonds Church Smiles*

Official Referees' Business [1995] 1 EGLR 155

An award under the Act is not an arbitration award; it is *sui generis*[1] and more in the nature of an expert determination

The court has wide powers to alter any award and to do so must have the power to substitute its own finding or conclusion for any finding or conclusion that the surveyor(s) made or may be presumed to have made.

The statutory scheme is intended to provide a relatively inexpensive method of resolving differences.

The Act envisages that if three surveyors are to be appointed, a party-appointed surveyor while no doubt retaining his professional independence is not obliged to act without regard to the interests of the party who appointed him.

Woodhouse v *Consolidated Property Corporation Ltd*

Court of Appeal [1993]1 EGLR 174

A matter which arises during the carrying out of the works, about which there is a dispute, must be a matter which relates to the consent

---

[1]   Latin phrase meaning "of its own right". Something in class of its own.

for the works to be carried out, eg whether the building owner is complying with a particular requirement in the consent. Section 55 does not permit or authorise the surveyor appointed under this part of the 1939 Act to determine other disputes arising between the parties.

It follows, in my judgment, that under the 1939 Act Mr Poole had no jurisdiction to make the award which he purported to make. Mr Poole's award in this action is evidence, but no more.

Reported third surveyor cases

Chartered Society of Physiotherapy v Simmonds Church Smiles

OFFICIAL REFEREES' BUSINESS

January 24 1995
JUDGE HUMPHREY LLOYD QC
Estates Gazette April 8 1995 [1995] 1 EGLR 155

London Building Acts (Amendment) Act 1939 — Appeal from surveyor's award — Whether appellate court entitled to receive additional evidence not before surveyor — Whether appellate court's jurisdiction limited

In October 1987 the appellant society served notice under the London Building Acts (Amendment) Act 1939 on the respondent firm that it proposed certain building works, which would affect the party wall between their respective properties. The two surveyors, who were appointed by each party respectively, made an award by which the appellant had liberty to demolish and reconstruct the party wall subject to certain conditions. Following the works the respondents claimed that their building had suffered damage and the two surveyors appointed a third surveyor who made an award identifying the appellant's works as the prime cause of movement to the respondents' property; the award also contained directions if the parties' surveyors could not agree the quantum of damages. On

October 27 1993 the appellant appealed that award to the county court under section 55(n)(i) of the Act contending that the third surveyor was wrong in finding that its works caused damage to the respondents' property. The appeal was transferred to the High Court as official referees' business where, at a hearing of certain preliminary questions and issues, the respondent argued that the power of the court on an appeal under section 55(n)(i) was limited and additional evidence not before the third surveyor could not be admitted.

Held: **On an appeal under section 55(n)(i) of the 1939 Act the court has jurisdiction in order, if required, to rescind or to modify an award in such manner as it thinks fit and for that purpose to receive any evidence (whether of fact or opinion) relevant to an issue raised by the appeal, including evidence which was not or could not have been available to the surveyor(s) when the award was made. On an appeal under section 55(n)(ii) and (o) the High Court has the same jurisdiction and powers in relation to any issue before it. The appellant was entitled to pursue an appeal under section 55(n)(ii), although in fact the appeal was before the High Court, following transfer from the county court, under section 55(n)(i). One could not conclude from section 55(a) to (l) (if it were necessary to reach a decision) that an award under the Act was an arbitration award; it is sui generis and more in the nature of an expert determination. Section 55(m) plainly excludes the Arbitration Acts. The award was one which may be completely reopened if an appeal is made; the court has wide powers to alter any award and to do so must have the power to substitute its own finding or conclusion for any finding or conclusion that the surveyor presumed to have made. Essentially, the question the court has to resolve is what award ought now to be made, taking into account all the facts established by admissible evidence, rather than the narrow question as to whether the award was made by a competent surveyor.**

The following case is referred to in this report.

Ladd v *Marshall* [1954] 1 WLR 1489; [1954] 3 All ER 745, CA

This was the hearing of certain preliminary questions and issues ordered to be heard on a summons for directions in an appeal made by Chartered Society of Physiotherapy, under section 55(n)(i) of the London Building Acts (Amendment) Act 1939 from a decision of a surveyor appointed under the Act, to Clerkenwell County Court, which had been transferred to the High Court under section 42 of the County Courts Act 1981 to which Simmonds Church Smiles was respondent.

Jonathan Howard (instructed by Mackrell Turner Garrett) appeared for the appellant; Benjamin Levy (instructed by Simmonds Church Smiles) represented the respondent.

Giving judgment, JUDGE HUMPHREY LLOYD QC said: Chartered Society of Physiotherapy (the appellant) occupies 14 Jockey's Fields,[1] WC1 and is its building owner for the purposes of Part VI of the London Building Acts (Amendment) Act 1939 (the Act). Simmonds Church Smiles (the respondent) is a firm of solicitors and is the adjoining owner (as defined by the Act) of the premises next door at 13 Jockey's Fields. In October 1987 the appellant served notice on the respondent of its intention to reconstruct its premises which necessitated work to the party wall with the respondent's premises. The appellant appointed Mr J E S Webb FRICS to act as its surveyor under the statutory procedure (to which I shall later refer) and the respondent (which dissented from the appellant's notice) appointed Mr J B Anderson FRICS as its surveyor.

The two surveyors met and inspected the premises and made an award dated (surprisingly) December 25 1988 by virtue of which the appellant was permitted to demolish the party wall and to construct a new wall. The appellant's liberty granted by the award was made conditional on compliance with a number of conditions both special and general. In para 2 it was recorded that:

It was agreed that in executing these works the following measures or construction will be implemented:

(a)   That the works will be executed in such a manner as not to impose any stress sufficient to cause damage on the existing retained structure of the adjoining premises.

Para 4 provided:

That if the Building Owner exercises the above rights he shall:

---

1   Jockey's Fields in so far it runs parallel to Bedford Row was known in the C18 as Bedford Row Mews and until relatively recently retained the character of a mews. (John Abernethy the founder of the Medical School at St Bartholemew's Hospital lived at 14 Bedford Row.)

(b) Take all reasonable precautions and provide all necessary support to retain the Adjoining Owner's land and buildings.

(c) Make good forthwith all structural, decorative and other damage to the Adjoining Owner's buildings occasioned by the said works in materials to match existing works, the extent of the said damage to be established by reference to the Schedule of Condition (which was attached to the Award).

(d) That the Building Owner shall be liable for and shall indemnify the Adjoining Owners against any justified expense, liability, loss, claim, or proceedings whatsoever arising under statute or at common law in respect of injury to or the death of any person or damage to property caused by, or in consequence of, the execution of the said works.

The award further provided:

7. That the works shall be carried through with reasonable expedition after commencement and so as to avoid any unnecessary inconvenience to the Adjoining Owner or occupiers.

9. That the said Surveyors reserve the right to make and issue any further Award or Awards that may be necessary, as provided in the said Acts.

The appellant went ahead with the rebuilding of 14 Jockey's Fields. It seems that the work affected the respondent's adjacent property at 13 Bedford Row[2] for it was alleged that it had thereby suffered settlement and consequential damage. This was not accepted by Mr Webb so the two surveyors referred the matter to Mr John Anstey FRICS, who had been appointed by them as the third surveyor under the Act.

Mr Anstey inspected the site, listened to the parties' surveyors, read and considered reports, drawings and photographs and on October 13 1993 made an award in which he decided:

The prime cause of the movement of the rear addition of 13 Bedford Row was the works undertaken to 14 Jockey's Fields/Bedford Row.

I have, as yet, formed no firm conclusion as to the extent of the works necessary for remedying the defects and damage caused by the settlement, but I should indicate to both surveyors that I am inclined to the view that the element of betterment is higher than the figure quoted by the Adjoining

---

2 Gillian Bebbington in London Street Names (1972) suggests that the name owes its origin to its use in the C16 when the Lord Mayor and aldermen rode ceremonially to inspect the City conduit beside the Tyburn River. However, Bedford Row was so named as it stood on hunting land given to Bedford Grammar School by Sir William Harper (when Lord Mayor).

Owner's surveyor. If, therefore, the two surveyors are unable to agree upon quantum, I would invite them to submit further argument to me on that subject.

I hereby direct that, within 14 days after the 14 days for appeal against this award shall have run, the two surveyors shall endeavour to reach agreement on quantum. Failing such agreement, they shall make submissions to me within a further 14 days, and within 7 days after receipt of each other's submissions they shall submit their respective comments thereon to me.

On October 27 1993 the appellant lodged an appeal in Clerkenwell County Court. The material grounds of appeal were set out in para 2 (the first ground is no longer pursued):

(a)   The Third Surveyor, not being himself a qualified civil engineer, made his award without obtaining the assistance of an expert civil engineering assessor

(b)   The Third Surveyor made his award without taking any or any adequate account of the opinion, expressed by Martin Moore of Ellis and Moore, expert civil engineer in written reports dated September 1992 and September 1993

(c)   The Third Surveyor erred in finding as fact that:

   (i)   the defects in the rear extension to No 13 Jockey's Fields complained of by the Respondents were caused by the works carried out by the Applicant to No 14 Jockey's Fields covered by the party wall award bearing the date 25 December 1988 ...

   (ii)   the remedial works carried out by the Respondents in 1992 and 1993 were reasonably necessary to remedy defects caused as aforesaid

(d)   Alternatively, the Third Surveyor's said findings were contrary to the weight of the evidence.

The appeal was transferred (by virtue of section 42 of the County Courts Act 1984) to the High Court as official referees' business on May 25 1994. The appellant sought directions in the usual way. Mr Benjamin Levy, for the respondent, made it clear that it would be argued that the court's powers on the appeal were limited. This contention was not accepted by the appellant. Since its outcome would affect the appropriate directions that would need to be given I adjourned the summons for directions to December 19 1994 and ordered that the following questions or issues should then be determined:

(A) What is the extent of the court's jurisdiction and the nature of its investigation including the extent to which evidence not before the third surveyor can be admitted:
   (i) under section 55(n)(i) of the London Buildings Acts (Amendment) Act 1939;
   (ii) under section 55(n)(ii) of the London Buildings Acts (Amendment) Act 1939;
(B) Whether the appellant is entitled to prosecute an appeal under section 55(n)(ii).

Part VI of the Act allows a building owner in London, if he complies with its provisions, to enter his neighbour's land and to carry out operations and thus to avoid liability in tort for trespass or nuisance. Its provisions continued a policy that had been established for a long time and in practice the statutory scheme has proved to be very successful. Some measure of its success may be seen by the paucity of cases on the interpretation of the Act or of its predecessors. Counsel told me that they had been unable to find any authority relevant to the determination of the issues set out above. This suggests that awards made under the Act rarely reach the courts on appeal.

Sections 45 and 46 of the Act set out the rights available to owners of contiguous properties. Sections 47 and 48 make it incumbent on an owner to serve a party structure notice and entitle the adjoining owner to serve a counter-notice. Section 49 provides that unless there is consent to the party structure notice or to the counter-notice there is deemed to be dissent and a difference between the parties. Sections 50 and 52 also require notices to be given for certain further measures.

Section 55 deals with the settlement of differences. It states (so far is relevant to the issues):

> Where a difference arises or is deemed to have arisen between a building owner and an adjoining owner in respect of any matter connected with any work to which this Part of this Act relates the following provisions shall have effect:

— Paras (a) to (j) then deal with the appointment of surveyors and a third surveyor and the making of awards and I refer later to certain of them —

(k) The award may determine the right to execute and the time and manner of executing any work and generally any other matter arising out of or incidental to the difference ...

(m) The award shall be conclusive and shall not except as provided by this section be questioned in any court;

(n) Either of the parties to the difference may within fourteen days after the delivery of an award made under this section appeal to the county court against the award and the following provisions shall have effect:

    (i) Subject as hereafter in this paragraph provided the county court may rescind the award or modify it in such manner and make such order as to costs as it thinks fit;

    (ii) If the appellant against the award on appearing before the county court is unwilling that the matter should be decided by that court and satisfies that court that he will if the matter is decided against him be liable to pay a sum exclusive of costs exceeding one hundred pounds and gives security approved by the county court to prosecute his appeal in the High Court and to abide the event thereof all proceedings in the county court shall be stayed and the appellant may bring an action in the High Court against the other party to the difference;

(o) Where an appellant against an award brings an action in the High Court in pursuance of the last preceding paragraph the following provisions shall have effect:

    (i) If the parties agree as to the facts a special case may be stated for the opinion of the court and may be dealt with in accordance with or as nearly as circumstances admit in accordance with the rules of the court;

    (ii) In any other case the plaintiff in the action shall deliver to the defendant an issue whereby the matters in difference may be tried;

    (iii) The issue shall be in such form as may be agreed between the parties or in case of dispute ... as may be settled by the court;

    (iv) The action shall proceed and the issue shall be tried in accordance with or as nearly as circumstances admit in accordance with the rules of the court;

The respondent's first submission was that as a result of the transfer from county court there was before the court the appeal which was formerly before the county court, and not the type of proceedings in the High Court for which provision made in section 55(o) of the Act. Although it would therefore be technically open to this court to apply section 55(n)(ii) (as the conditions there set out would be satisfied since the appellant was insured and the value of any award was clearly going to be over £100) and thus to stay the proceedings and to require fresh proceedings to be brought in the High Court, it would not be sensible to do so. The respondent is clearly right in this submission and for practical purposes issue (B) disappears, but it will be answered in the affirmative. I did not understand the appellant to submit to the contrary once it became clear that the respondent accepted that the appeal was before the High Court, by virtue of the transfer, as an appeal under section 55(n)(i).

The respondent's principal submissions were however directed to the nature of the appeal. Its case was that an award is made conclusive by section 55(m) and, with one exception, the court's powers on appeal were akin to those of the Court of Appeal hearing an appeal from the High Court after a trial of fact and law so that, for example, no new evidence could be admitted which was not before who ever made the award. The exception related only to evidence to enable the court to know what might have been seen on site prior to the award where work had subsequently been carried out. These submissions in turn require a consideration of the nature of an award under the Act for that may determine the ambit of an appeal.

It is, in my judgment, clear from the general framework of the Act and particularly from the provisions relating to notices, counter-notices and how a difference is deemed to arise, that it is expected that the exercise of a right will be agreed. Indeed for this purpose the time for giving a counter-notice is in practice frequently extended by agreement. If a difference arises (and it cannot be resolved by agreement) then it is settled by the award of the agreed sole surveyor or, commonly in practice by the two surveyors appointed by the parties, or, if the third surveyor has to be brought in, by an award of any two of the three (see section 55(i)) or, if two surveyors cannot agree, then by an award of the third surveyor (section 55 (j)). In some respects the Act suggests that the difference is resolved by something in the nature of a statutory arbitration. The words 'difference', 'settle' and 'award' and the provisions for the appointment of a sole 'agreed surveyor' and for decisions by two of three surveyors or in default by the third surveyor are consistent with a judicial or quasi-judicial process. But the Act makes no provision for the parties to be heard or for the surveyor(s) to proceed as one might expect to proceed an arbitrator to act. Furthermore, the Act envisages that if three surveyors are to be appointed, a party-appointed surveyor while no doubt retaining his professional independence is not obliged to act without regard to the interests of the party who appointed him. In practice matters in difference are regularly resolved by agreement between the two party-appointed surveyors without the need for the intervention of the third surveyor. Thus, the Act works well. The relevant owner leaves it to the surveyor and has no need to prepare a case. The facts are elicited informally by inspection and by perusal of proposals and counterproposals, as probably happened in this case in 1988.

In the absence of authority I would not conclude from section 55(a) to (l) (if it were necessary to reach a decision) that an award under the Act was an arbitration award. An award under the Act is, in my judgment, *sui generis* and is more in the nature of an expert determination. The Act does not require the award to be a 'speaking' award and there is no apparent obligation for the award to contain findings of fact or conclusions of law and, of course, awards are customarily and commendably direct and to the point. Furthermore, section 55(m) plainly excludes the Arbitration Acts.

Mr Levy submitted that a purposive construction should be given to paras (n) and (o) and that 'appeal' meant therefore what he called a 'true appeal' as opposed to an appeal by way of rehearing, ie the appellant would have to satisfy the appellate court that the surveyor(s) had conducted the inquiry in such a way or had reached a result which could be shown to be wrong by the application of the principles which govern appeals to the Court of Appeal. Para (m) in permitting an award which was otherwise conclusive to be 'questioned' did not contemplate the appellate court conducting its own investigation. In particular the appellate court should not receive evidence which was not before the surveyor(s): the principles in *Ladd* v *Marshall* [1954] 1 WLR 1489 should apply. Mr Jonathan Howard argued to the contrary. He submitted that a court would have to have some evidence as to what was the situation in which a right was sought to be exercised, and if what was being questioned required a determination about a matter which the surveyor had found or concluded or which he ought to have found or concluded, a court ought to be able to determine whether 'new' evidence should be admitted. It was contrary to the interests of the parties and to the public interest that a question relating to an award should be decided on an erroneous or incomplete basis. In any event an appeal only required the court to reconsider that part of the award which was being questioned and not necessarily the whole award: see the procedure to be adopted under section 55(o).

Looking at the whole of section 55(n) and (o) it is, in my judgment, clear that the award is one which may be completely reopened if an appeal is duly made. Section 55(n)(i) provides that the county court may, '... modify it in such manner and make such order as to costs as it thinks fit'. In my view, the words, 'as it thinks fit' plainly qualify 'modify in such manner' and are not limited to an 'order as to costs' for otherwise 'such manner' is left hanging in the air. Thus, the court has, in my judgment, wide powers to alter any award and to do so must have the power to substitute its own finding or conclusion for any finding or conclusion that the surveyor(s) made or may be presumed to have made.

There is nothing in the Act to suggest that an appellant who satisfied section 55(n)(ii) would be unable to obtain from the High Court on appeal a result which could be obtained in the county court or vice versa. On the contrary if the appeal were substantial enough to warrant being heard in the High Court there is every reason to conclude that under the procedure for the trial of issues the High Court should be able to arrive at a result at least as favourable to the appellant as that which the county court had power to achieve under section 55(n)(i). By the same token if the appellant is entitled to have an issue tried in the High Court he must be able to do the same in the county court. Counsel helpfully pointed out that until very recently (and certainly at the date of the Act) there were statutory restrictions on transfers from the county court which would have precluded an appellant reaching the High Court without the special provisions of the kind set out in section 55(n) and (o) and they accounted for the form of section 55(o). Nevertheless it is, in my judgment, clear that although section 55(o) begins in subpara (i) by describing a procedure akin to an appeal on a question of law by way of case stated, eg by a special case under section 9 of the Arbitration Act 1934, it continues by making provision for the appellant to obtain a full-scale trial of whatever has to be determined to enable the appellant to succeed. Mr Howard drew attention to subpara (ii), which refers to the plaintiff delivering an issue 'whereby the matters in difference may be tried'. In my judgment, he was correct to submit that the words emphasised referred back to the earlier occasions where 'difference' was used (eg the opening words of the section and paras (b), (c), (d), (i), (k) and (n)) and showed that the intention of the Act was that an appellant could reopen any matter in difference, which had otherwise been conclusively resolved by the award. Therefore the court (whether county court or High Court) has, in my judgment, the power, if the appellant brings himself within the Act, to question anything decided by the award and to substitute its own decision.

This conclusion does not of course dispose of the respondent's principal submission that although the court may have wide powers they are nevertheless appellate and an appellant is therefore subject to the same limitations as an appellant in the High Court. Mr Levy persuasively submitted that since the court is not a qualified surveyor it did not make sense for there to be a complete rehearing which is a course that is acceptable where an appeal lies to someone just as well qualified as the original tribunal, eg to a county court or a High Court judge in chambers. An appellant ought not to be able to go over all the ground again before a less qualified tribunal. Accordingly, an appellant must be limited to the material before the original tribunal. Mr Howard pointed out that there was no such limitation in the Act and it would be contrary to the interests of justice as between the parties that an appellant should be so limited, particularly since the nature of the process by which the award was made was not like a trial in the county court or High Court (or like a hearing in an arbitration).

I do not consider that Mr Levy's submissions are right. First, as I have concluded, there is no necessary limitation in the statute on the powers of the court. Second, if, as Mr Levy accepted, the court may have to be put in the picture by receiving evidence about what was seen or to be seen by the surveyor(s) there must be some evidence before the court which was not given (in ordinary sense) to the original tribunal. Since in many (and probably) the majority of cases this evidence is likely to come from a professional person it seems to me to be unrealistic to suppose that such evidence will be purely factual. If the issue related to the condition of a party wall or chimney, evidence confined to the extent of weathering without some assessment of its effect would be of little real value.

Third, para (o)(iv) clearly envisages that in the High Court there would be a trial of such an issue (ie as to what was there to be seen), which is to be conducted 'in accordance with or as nearly as circumstances admit in accordance with the rules of the court'. Thus, in my judgment, the issue will be tried as an original action and will not be re-examined as if the High Court were the Court of Appeal. There will therefore be a 'rehearing' of that issue. The same must apply in the county court. It must be remembered that the appeal will only be concerned with that aspect of the award which is questioned and not with the whole of the original difference. This may of course mean that a court will receive evidence about a matter of fact or opinion which was not available to whoever made the award, but which proves to be determinative of the appeal. I do not consider that it is a sufficient objection that the award might be rescinded or modified because of evidence (or arguments which might have been but were not) considered by the surveyor(s). If it were it would mean a building owner might (or might not be) able to exercise a right or an adjoining owner might or might not be able to object to such rights being exercised or be otherwise prejudiced. That cannot be right. There are sufficient powers available to a court (eg by orders as to costs) to ensure that a party is not necessarily prejudiced if ultimately the appeal succeeds on grounds not available to the original tribunal.

Fourth, Mr Levy's submissions assume that there is some record of what the original tribunal had before it. All that may have happened is that a surveyor ('agreed' or 'third') visited the site and made a short non-speaking award which referred only to the building owner's proposal and to the counter-notice. The procedure would be investigatory and not necessarily 'adversarial'. I do not believe that the Parliament envisaged that, on an appeal, the court would first be asked to decide what evidence might be adduced to reconstruct the situation obtaining at the time of the award so as to provide the 'record' which would then set the scene for the appeal and for further argument as to whether 'new' evidence might be admitted. Such a procedure would be unnecessarily costly and contrary to the statutory scheme which is self-evidently intended to provide a relatively inexpensive method of resolving differences. If there is to be an appeal — and as I have already noted it seems rare for appeals to be pursued to a hearing — I am sure that the best and most efficacious course would be to enable the court to be as fully informed as possible about the point or points at issue and not to proceed on an artificial basis shutting out relevant facts or opinions merely because they were not before the original tribunal, even if they might have been available to it.

A fortiori if, for example, during the course of the work facts are discovered which if they had been known to the original tribunal might have affected the award, it does not, in my judgment, make any sense to exclude those facts from the evidence before the court hearing an appeal. Essentially the question which the court has to resolve is what award ought now to be made, taking into account all the facts established by admissible evidence, rather the narrow question contended for by the respondent which is close to an investigation as to whether the award was made by a competent surveyor or surveyors. Depending on the point or points at issue on the appeal there may have to be a rehearing. As I have stated that indeed is, in my judgment, exactly what is envisaged by section 55(o)(iv).

Accordingly, the questions or issues are to be answered as follows:

(A)(i) On appeal under section 55(n)(i) of the Act the county court and this court by virtue of the transfer to it of the appeal before the county court has jurisdiction in order, if required, to rescind or to modify an award in such manner as it thinks fit and for that purpose to receive any evidence (whether of fact or opinion) relevant to an issue raised by the appeal, including evidence which was not or could not have been available to the surveyor(s) when the award was made.

(ii) On an appeal under section 55(n)(ii) and (o) of the Act the High Court has the same jurisdiction and powers in relation to any issue before it.

(B) Yes.

Woodhouse v *Consolidated Property Corporation Ltd*

COURT OF APPEAL
November 3 1992
Before Lord Justice GLIDEWELL and Lord Justice Simon BROWN
[1993] 1 EGLR 174

Party wall — Whether third surveyor appointed under London Building Acts (Amendment) Act 1939 had jurisdiction to make award determining responsibility for collapse of party wall

Ord 14 summons — Whether condition that defendants pay into court £350,000 before leave to defend proper exercise of courts discretion

The plaintiff was the owner of 61 Endell Street, Covent Garden, London WC2, where he carried on a timber merchant's business, and on which stood a timber shed. The defendants were the owners of the adjoining premises, a former mission hall, the basement floor of which lay some 2.3m below the ground level of the timber yard. In 1990 the defendants commenced building works to the mission hall, including lowering the basement floor. On January 14 1991 the defendant gave the plaintiff a notice under section 47 of the London Building Acts (Amendment) Act 1939 of their intention to carry out work to the wall of the mission hall on the boundary of the properties. On January 25 1991, before the expiration of the 14 days provided by the Act for the giving of consent, the wall of the mission hall on the boundary collapsed and seriously damaged the timber-storage shed. Following the appointment by the parties of surveyors under the 1939 Act, the two surveyors appointed a third surveyor. The plaintiff commenced the present action by the issue of the writ on December 10 1991 claiming damages for nuisance and trespass; the damages included £430,000 for the cost of rebuilding the timber shed and loss of profits continuing at £2,660 per month. By an award of December 10 1991 the third surveyor determined that the prime cause of the collapse was the defendants' work for which they were responsible. On June 15 1992 the plaintiff issued a summons for summary judgment under RSC Ord 14 and on June 27 1992 the plaintiff sought leave to amend the statement of claim with a pleading that by the third surveyor's award the defendants were estopped from denying that they were responsible for the collapse of the wall. At the hearing of the summons Judge Hordern QC (sitting as a judge of the High Court) gave leave to amend the statement of claim and granted the defendants leave to defend on condition that £350,000 be paid into court within 14 days. The defendant appealed against both orders contending that if the statement of claim were to be amended there should be an adjournment of the Ord 14 summons.

Held: **The appeal was dismissed. Where an amendment to a statement of claim is allowed, then formally the plaintiff should have taken out a fresh summons under Ord 14 and in the circumstances an adjournment should have been granted. However, as the defendants had had sufficient time to consider the amendments, and had produced additional affidavit evidence, the court would formally dismiss the defendants' appeal against the amendment and hear the appeal against the judge's further order as if a fresh Ord 14 summons had been issued.**

Under the 1939 Act the third surveyor had no jurisdiction to make the award he purported to make because section 55 of the Act, which provides for the resolution of disputes between adjoining owners, is limited to the resolution of disputes between adjoining owners, as to whether one of them shall be permitted under the Act to carry out works the subject of a notice under section 47, and if so, the terms and conditions. Section 55 of the Act does not permit or authorise the surveyor appointed under the Act to determine other disputes arising between the parties. Having regard to the other causes of action relied on by the plaintiff, the judge was correct in giving leave to defend and in saying that he could almost give judgment for the plaintiff in justifying the condition for a payment into court. Having regard to the likely total claim of the plaintiff, the sum ordered as a condition for giving leave to defend cannot be said to be wrong.

The following cases are referred to in this report.

Dalton v *Angus* (1881) 6 App Cas 740; [1881] All ER Repl; 50 LJQB 689; 44 LT 844; 46 JP 132; 30 WR 191, HL
Ladd v *Marshall* [1954] 1 WLR 1489; [1954] 3 All ER 745, CA
Wringe v *Cohen* [1940] 1 KB 229

This was an appeal by the defendants, and a cross-appeal by the plaintiff, from orders of Judge Hordern QC (sitting as a judge of the High Court) who, on the hearing the plaintiff's summons seeking leave to amend his statement of claim and for summary judgment under RSC Ord 14, had granted the plaintiff leave to amend and granted the defendants leave to defend on condition that they first paid into court £350,000. Bruce Mauleverer QC and Mark Raeside (instructed by Beachcroft Stanleys) appeared for the appellant/defendants; Stephen Hockman QC and Adrian Jack (instructed by Barrett & Co, of Reading) represented the respondent/plaintiff.

Giving judgment, GLIDWELL LJ said: The plaintiff, Mr Woodhouse, owns and occupies 61 Endell Street, Covent Garden, London WC2, and a yard behind that building. At those premises he carried on business as a timber merchant, trading as Latchfords (Endell Street). The business is long-established. Mr Woodhouse himself has been in the business since 1953, at first as an employee, then as a partner and latterly as sole proprietor.

The defendants, the appellants in this court, are the owners of 68a Neal Street, Covent Garden. This property is a former mission hall, approached only by a narrow pedestrian passage from Neal Street, which runs parallel to Endell Street. The north-easterly wall of the mission hall lies immediately adjacent to the south-westerly boundary of the plaintiff's timber yard. In the timber yard, immediately adjacent to the wall of the mission hall, there was a storage shed for timber. This structure consisted of five brick pillars, three adjoining the wall of the mission hall, two at the north-easterly side, with a monopitch roof at the same height as the roof of the mission hall.

The mission hall had ground and first floors and a basement. The floor of the basement lay some distance – one report says approximately 2.3m – below the ground level of the timber yard. Thus, in practice, the wall of the mission hall, below the ground floor of that structure, acted as a retaining wall for the timber yard and the soil beneath it.

In the autumn of 1990 the defendants commenced works on the mission hall, which included lowering the floor of the basement. There is a dispute as to what stage those works had reached, and the condition of the building, at the relevant date.

On January 14 1991 the defendants served on the plaintiff a notice under the London Building Acts (Amendment) Act 1939, section 47, of their intention to carry out works to the wall of the mission hall on the boundary of the properties. It is agreed that the wall was a party wall within the definition in section 44 of the 1939 Act. The works referred to in the notice included 'underpinning and reinforced concrete retaining wall'. In accordance with the Act, the notice provided that if within 14 days the plaintiff did not consent to the works, he was deemed to have dissented. In that case a difference would have arisen between the parties under the relevant part of the 1939 Act. The notice said that it was intended to commence works earlier than the expiration of the 14 days by agreement. As I have already said, the works had commenced some time previously and according to the defendants the underpinning was substantially complete.

On January 25 1991, ie before the expiration of the 14 days under the notice, the wall of the mission hall adjoining the timber yard collapsed. Initially there was a suggestion that the collapse was towards the mission hall, but it now appears that the experts are agreed that above ground level the collapse was into the timber yard. In collapsing, the wall seriously damaged the timber-storage shed.

Both the plaintiff and the defendants appointed surveyors to act for them in the dispute which had arisen under the Act of 1939. The plaintiff appointed Mr Paul Cackett [BSc] FRICS, and the defendants, Mr Andrew Halstead [BSc] ARICS. They, in turn, appointed a third surveyor to resolve the dispute, Mr Anthony Poole, [FRICS ACIArb]. He signed an award on December 10 1991. One of the issues in this appeal concerns the validity of that award, to which I shall have to return.

The action

The plaintiff issued his writ on December 10 1991. It claimed damages against the defendants for nuisance, trespass to land, trespass to goods and negligence. The statement of claim was served on February 5 1992. In its original form it made no reference to the award of Mr Poole under the 1939 Act. In the particulars of special damage, the major item was the cost of rebuilding, which was put at some £403,000. Damages were also claimed for loss of profit of the business and additional expenses at the rate of £2,660 per month, together with a number of smaller items.

The defendants filed their defence on April 14 1992. On June 15 1992 the plaintiffs solicitors took out a summons for judgment under RSC Ord 14, and for an order for an interim payment, and for speedy trial of the action. The date for the hearing of these applications was fixed before a judge for July 30 1992. On July 27 1992 the plaintiff's solicitors took out a summons for leave to amend the statement of claim, which was served on the defendants' solicitors on July 28 1992. The defendants also made an application for an order striking out parts of an affidavit sworn by Mr Woodhouse in support of his application for judgment under Ord 14.

The applications were heard by Judge Hordern QC, sitting as a High Court judge, on July 30 1992. He ordered that the plaintiff should have leave to amend his statement of claim, with consequent leave to the defendants to amend their defence. He refused an application by counsel for the defendants to adjourn the hearing of the application for summary judgment under Ord 14. On that application he granted the defendants leave to defend on condition that within 14 days they paid into court the sum of £350,000. He made no order on the defendants' application with regard to Mr Woodhouse's affidavit.

The defendants now appeal to this court against both orders made by the judge. By a subsequent order of this court, compliance with the condition requiring payment into court has been stayed, pending the hearing of this appeal.

The appeal against the order for amendment of the statement of claim

The major amendment was the addition of four paragraphs following para 10. The first three of these paragraphs read:

10a. By an award dated 10 December 1991, lawfully made by Anthony Poole, the third surveyor duly appointed pursuant to the London Building Acts (Amendment) Act 1939 to resolve a difference arising between the plaintiff and the defendant herein, namely the responsibility for the cost of rebuilding the wall and certain related fees, it was determined:
(a) that the prime cause of the collapse pleaded in paragraph 6 hereof was work being carried out by the defendant; and
(b) that the defendant was responsible for the collapse of the wall as pleaded in paragraph 6 hereof; and
(c) that the defendants should pay the costs of the plaintiff's surveyor and of the third surveyor in the said reference.

10b. No appeal has been made from the said award.

10c. In the premises the defendant is estopped per rem judicatam from denying that it is responsible for the said collapse.

Para 10d sets out the additional costs which it is alleged have not been satisfied by the defendants. The amendments also include an allegation that the collapse of the wall was caused by the defendants 'failing timeously to service Notices under the London Building Acts'.

At the hearing before Judge Hordern, the defendants did not oppose the amendment as such, but sought an adjournment if that amendment were to be granted. It was argued on their behalf that formally the plaintiff's solicitors, after amending their statement of claim if leave were granted, should take out a fresh summons under Ord 14, thus giving the defendants the opportunity to file evidence in reply to the allegations in the amended statement of claim. Counsel for the defendants argued that if the judge did not grant an adjournment, he should consider the Ord 14 application only on the material before him which related to the statement of claim in its original form.

In my judgment, these submissions by counsel for the defendants were correct. The judge apparently took the view that in seeking an adjournment the defendants were merely trying to delay the resolution of the dispute. But the plaintiff, by his amendment, was making a major change in the basis of his claim. I agree that if such amendment were to be permitted (and there was no good reason why it should not have been) then formally the plaintiff should have taken out a fresh summons under Ord 14. No doubt it was permissible to waive this formality by treating the original summons as applying to the amended statement of claim, but if that were to be done, the defendants should have been granted an adjournment and the opportunity to file further evidence. I appreciate that the judge's decision in this respect was one made in the exercise of his discretion, but, in my view, he exercised that discretion on a wholly wrong basis.

This raised the question, what should we now do in this court in relation to this appeal? By now the defendants and their advisers have had ample time to consider the amended statement of claim. They have filed an amended defence on August 24 1992. Moreover, the defendants seek leave to adduce further evidence at the hearing of this appeal, namely a further affidavit from Mr B G McCarthy, the defendants' solicitor, sworn on October 5 1992, to which is exhibited a further report from Mr A G Antrobus. Mr Antrobus, whose qualifications are not stated in his report, is a member or employee of the Brian Clancy

Partnership, chartered engineers and civil and structural engineers.

After some discussion Mr Bruce Mauleverer QC, for the appellants, agreed that provided we gave leave for the additional evidence to be adduced, there would now be no disadvantage to his clients in the amendment of the statement of claim, and thus the main appeal could proceed as if the Ord 14 summons had been issued after the amendment of pleadings.

However, Mr Stephen Hockman QC for the plaintiff/respondent, then submitted that in considering whether to admit the further evidence, we were obliged to apply the principles derived from *Ladd* v *Marshall* [1954] 1 WLR 1489. In particular, the further report from Mr Antrobus, which it is sought to adduce, could have been available before the hearing before Judge Hordern and thus should not be admitted in evidence.

RSC Ord 59, r 10(2) provides:

> The Court of Appeal shall have power to receive further evidence on questions of fact, either by oral examination in court, by affidavit . . . but, in the case of an appeal from a judgment after trial or hearing of any cause or matter on the merits, no such further evidence (other than evidence as to matters which have occurred after the date of the trial or hearing) shall be admitted except on special grounds.

It is commonplace that the principles in *Ladd* v *Marshall* define the special grounds for admitting such further evidence.

The essential question therefore is, the judge having granted the defendants leave to appeal on condition of a payment into court, has there been a trial or hearing of the action on the merits? The current edition of the Supreme Court Practice (1993 ed) contains the following note, numbered 59/10/8:

> It was held in *Langdale* v *Danby* [1982] 1 WLR 1123; [1982] 3 All ER 129, HL that a judgment given under O14 (or O86) was a judgment given after a hearing on the merits; it follows that the Ladd v Marshall conditions apply where there is an application to adduce further evidence in an appeal against such a judgment (*Lodge Green Limited* v *Leitch (trading as Manx Electronics)*, November 2 1982 (unrep), CA and *K/S/A/S Oil Transport* v *Saudi Research and Development Corporation Ltd* [1984] 1 Lloyd's Rep 5, CA). But an order refusing summary judgment or granting conditional leave to defend is not an order made after a hearing on the merits (see below).
>
> In *Wellery Dunbar*, January 27 1984, CA (unrep) it was held that an order setting aside a default judgment is not a decision after a 'hearing on the

merits' (even though the merits are taken into account in deciding whether to set aside the default judgment), because the hearing on the merits in the shape of the trial of the action is yet to come. It is submitted that the same reasoning applies where an application for summary judgment is refused, or conditional leave to defend is granted, and therefore the Ladd v Marshall conditions do not have to be satisfied in such cases .. .

I have set out this reasoning because I entirely agree with it and I need add no words of my own. It follows that the defendants do not need to show 'special grounds' for the admission of the fresh evidence in this case and the *Ladd* v *Marshall* principles do not apply.

It was for these reasons that at this stage in the hearing we announced that we would formally dismiss the appeal against the judge's order allowing the amendment to the pleadings, and would proceed to hear the main appeal as if the Ord 14 summons had been taken out after those amendments had been completed and the further evidence had been filed.

The issues

The original statement of claim in essence alleged three causes of action. These were:

(i)   negligence;
(ii) simple nuisance;
(iii) breach of an easement of support, for which the right of action is also in nuisance.

The amended statement of claim pleaded that, as a result of Mr Poole's award, the defendants were estopped from denying that they were responsible for the collapse of their wall. Clearly if this plea were established, the plaintiff would be entitled to judgment on the Ord 14 summons. I therefore propose to consider this plea as a fourth issue.

I will therefore consider each of these issues in turn.

(i) Negligence

Proof that the defendants, or those for whose acts they were responsible when negligent, depends upon proof of facts which are in issue between the parties. Mr Hockman accepts that this as a cause of action cannot be the basis of the judgment under Ord 14.

(ii) *Simple nuisance*

This cause of action is based upon the decision of this court in *Wringe* v *Cohen* [1940] 1 KB 229. At the commencement of his judgment, Judge Hordern said:

> In my view, without anything more, the plaintiff is clearly entitled to damages, for unless the wall fell from some act of a stranger, act of the plaintiff himself or some insidious cause which the defendants could not know about, then I think that Mr Hockman is right on the authority of *Wringe* v *Cohen* [1940] 1 KB 229 and, indeed, if I may say so without disrespect to the learned judge who decided that case, I would have thought also on pure matters of first principle the plaintiff would obviously have been entitled to succeed.

Wringe v *Cohen*, like the present case, was an action between the owners of two adjoining properties. The plaintiff was the owner of a shop which was substantially damaged when the gable end of the adjoining house, owned by the defendant, collapsed on to it during a storm. There was evidence that the gable wall had been in a state of disrepair for some years. The house was let to a tenant. There was an issue as to whether the defendant, as owner not in occupation, was liable for the damage caused by the collapse of the gable wall in the absence of proof that he knew or ought to have known of its state of disrepair.

Atkinson J, giving the judgment of the court, said at p233:

> In our judgment if, owing to want of repair, premises on a highway become dangerous and, therefore, a nuisance, and a passer-by or an adjoining owner suffers damage by their collapse, the occupier, or the owner if he has undertaken the duty of repair, is answerable whether he knew or ought to have known of the danger or not. The undertaking to repair gives the owner control of the premises, and a right of access thereto for the purpose of maintaining them in a safe condition. On the other hand, if the nuisance is created, not by want of repair, but, for example, by the act of a trespasser, or by a secret and unobservable operation of nature, such as a subsidence under or near the foundations of the premises, neither an occupier nor an owner responsible for repair is answerable, unless with knowledge or means of knowledge he allows the danger to continue. In such a case he has in no sense caused the nuisance by any act or breach of duty.

Although Atkinson J referred to the liability of an owner or occupier of premises on a highway, in that case it appears to have been irrelevant to the decision that the defendant's property was on a highway. Thus the decision appears to support the proposition that, if the wall of the mission hall collapsed due to want of repair, the defendants are liable in nuisance without proof that the defendants knew or should have known of the dangerous condition of the wall, unless it can be shown that the collapse was due either to the plaintiff's own act, to the act of a stranger or to some latent defect.

The decision in *Wringe* v *Cohen*, if it does establish the proposition I have just set out, has been much criticised. Mr Mauleverer submits that this proposition is not good law, in the sense that it is not supported by, or consistent with, other authorities.

Mr Hockman has saved us from deciding this interesting but difficult point by conceding that, as the defendants plead that in this case the collapse of their wall was caused by the plaintiff's own act, in order to secure a judgement under Ord 14 he has in practice to defeat that defence by proving what he requires to prove in order to establish nuisance by breach of an easement of support. It is therefore not necessary for us to consider the cause of action is simple nuisance further.

It is convenient to consider the next issue.

(iv) Estoppel by reason of the award of Mr Poole under the London Building Acts (Amendment) Act 1939

Under section 49 of the 1939 Act if an owner of land on whom a party structure notice under section 47 has been served does not consent in writing to the carrying out of the work specified in the notice, he is deemed to have dissented from the notice and 'a difference shall be deemed to have arisen between the parties'. Section 55 of the Act then contains a detailed procedure for settlement of such a difference. If, as here, each party appoints a surveyor and they do not agree, they must appoint a third surveyor.

So far as material, section 55(i) provides:

> The agreed surveyor . . . shall settle by award any matter which before the commencement of any work to which a Notice under this Part of this Act relates or from time to time during the continuance of such work may be in dispute between the building owner and the adjoining owner.

Section 55(k) provides:

> The award may determine the right to execute and the time and manner of

executing any work and generally any other matter arising out of or incidental to the difference.

In a letter to Mr Poole, dated April 23 1991, the plaintiff's surveyor, Mr Cackett, said:

The dispute concerns the responsibility of costs for reconstructing the party wall between the two properties, the associated costs arising from the collapse of the party wall, ie damages, surveyors' and engineers' fees, consequential losses and the reconstruction costs for Latchford's including all fees etc.

Mr Poole accepted the responsibility of determining the dispute so defined and in his award he provided:

1.   The building owner will pay the proper cost of rebuilding the party wall ... .
2.   The building owner will pay the proper cost of reconstructing those parts of the (plaintiffs) premises which were damaged or collapsed as a result of the collapse of the party wall.

Mr Mauleverer submits that Mr Poole had no jurisdiction to make such an award under the scheme of the 1939 Act. If that is correct, he further submits that the award would be of no effect and thus could not estop his clients in any way.

Although subpara (i) of section 55 requires the surveyor to settle by his award any matter which ... from time to time during the continuance of such work may be in dispute...', this must, in my view, be read in its context. The context in particular includes the provisions of subpara (k), which commences: The award may determine the right to execute and the time and manner of executing any work ...'. In my judgment, the provisions of section 55 relate only to the resolution of differences between adjoining owners as to whether one of them shall be permitted under the Act to carry out works, the subject of a section 47 notice, and if so, the terms and conditions under which he is permitted to carry out such work. A matter which arises during the carrying out of the works, about which there is a dispute, must therefore be a matter which relates to the consent for the works to be carried out, eg whether the building owner is complying with a particular requirement in the consent. Section 55 does not permit or authorise the surveyor appointed under this part of the 1939 Act to determine other disputes arising between the parties.

It follows, in my judgment, that under the 1939 Act Mr Poole had no jurisdiction to make the award which he purported to make. Mr Poole's award in this action is evidence, but no more. That is how the judge treated it in his judgment.

(iii) *Breach of the easement of support*

In para 5 of his statement of claim (which was not altered in the amendment) the plaintiff pleads as follows:

> The plaintiff and his predecessors in title have for upwards of forty years, alternatively twenty years, before 1 January 1987 and/or before 25 January 1991, enjoyed support from the wall and in the premises by virtue of the Prescription Act 1837... the plaintiff at all material times has enjoyed an easement of support from the wall.

By their amended defence, the defendants complain that this paragraph does not properly plead the nature of the easement of support which is claimed. It has been made clear during the hearing (if it was not clear before) that what the plaintiff claims is that he was entitled to support from the lower part of the defendants' wall for the land adjoining the wall forming part of his timber yard, and for the storage shed upon it, in its use as a shed for storing timber. In my view the pleading sufficiently covers this case, though I agree it could be more clearly set out in the statement of claim.

Apart from not admitting that such an easement exists, the defence in essence is that the collapse of the wall was caused, not by any failure on the defendants' part to continue to support the plaintiff's land and building, but as a result of the plaintiff bringing timber on his land which surcharged the land.

Mr Mauleverer submits that, as a matter of law, an easement of support if it has been created is for the support of the land and the building, but not for chattels, ie the timber on the land and in the building. In my judgment this is not a correct way to approach the issue. If an easement has been acquired by prescription, so that a plaintiff is entitled to enjoy support for his land and building from his neighbour's adjoining land or building, that right is for support for the land and building as they have been used during the period of prescription. Only if it can be shown that the nature of the use has materially altered can it be said that the easement does not benefit the plaintiff. We have not been referred to any authority in which this question has been raised directly, but, in my view, the proposition I have sought to set out is consistent with and follows the principles to be derived from the leading authority, *Dalton* v *Angus* (1881) 6 App Cas 740.

I consider next Mr Mauleverer's submission that the judge adopted a wrong approach when considering whether he should make leave to defend conditional upon the defendants' bringing a substantial sum into court.

It is a commonplace that if, on an application by a plaintiff under Ord 14 for summary judgment, the defendant persuades the court by his evidence that there is a triable issue, he should be given leave to defend. However, the courts are increasingly willing to make use of the power to grant such leave only subject to a condition requiring the defendant to pay money into court. The authorities on the grant of conditional leave are set out in some detail in the note in the *Supreme Court Practice*, 14/3–4/15, and I need not refer to them further.

In the decided cases, different expressions have been used to describe the circumstances in which a court is justified in imposing such a condition. The expressions most frequently used are that the court 'is prepared very nearly to give judgment for the plaintiff', or that the defence can properly be described as 'shadowy'. I do not detect any difference of substance between these expressions. Mr Mauleverer submits, and I agree, that for a defence properly to be described as 'shadowy', the court must have doubts about the defendants' good faith in advancing it. But the less likely a defence is to succeed, the easier it is for a court to infer that the defendant is seeking leave to defend for some ulterior reason, of which delay is the most obvious. Such a reason obviously casts doubt on the defendant's good faith.

In his judgment, the judge said:

> It seems to me that it is impossible for me to say on the affidavit evidence without actually trying this matter on reading experts' evidence, which I am certainly not anxious to do, that there is no triable issue.

We should not, in my view, disagree with that conclusion. It follows that I would dismiss the plaintiff's cross-appeal.

The judge also said:

> All those considerations lead me to think that it matters not how one puts it, though I think it is probably wrong to say the defence is shadowy because it is actually quite clear. It is just that its chances of success are less than ample, shall we say.

When, in the authorities, judges have in the past referred to a defence being 'shadowy', they have clearly, in my view, meant that it had little substance and perhaps that for this reason it was difficult to discern whether there really was a defence. They have not been referring to the clarity with which the defence was, or was not, pleaded. Thus in this sentence of his judgment I believe the judge was not using the word 'shadowy' in the sense in which it was used in the authorities.

Mr Mauleverer also submits that where a defendant has shown that he will be well able to meet any judgment which might be given, a condition of payment into court should not be imposed on granting leave to defend. For my part I am not prepared to accept, without further argument, that when a judge is prepared 'very nearly to give judgment for the plaintiff', he should nevertheless not impose a condition on granting leave to defend to a defendant who proves that he has ample resources to meet a judgment, while being willing to impose such a condition on a defendant of lesser means. However, in this case it is not necessary to decide whether this submission is correct, because on the material before us the defendants have not shown, to the necessary high standard, that they are at present well able to meet any judgment which they may have to meet.

Since I agree that the judge was correct in granting leave to defend, it is clearly inappropriate for me to rehearse the evidence as to the reasons why the wall collapsed. It suffices to say that, having considered that evidence, I am satisfied that the judge was right to say that he could 'almost give judgment for the plaintiff'. Accordingly, I also think that he was justified in imposing a requirement that the defendants should make a substantial payment into court as a precondition to the grant of such leave.

I note that the order actually made by the judge was:

> If the defendant within 14 days pays £350,000 into court he may defend the action as to the whole of the plaintiff's claim.

It is apparent that he intended that if the defendants failed to comply with the condition, they should not have leave to defend. However, in my view, the order should also say in terms that if the defendants fail to comply with the condition, within the specified time, the plaintiff should be entitled to sign judgment for damages to be assessed.

Quantum

This leaves only the question which is raised by the appeal as to whether the amount of £350,000, which the judge required to be paid into court, is excessive. The plaintiff's total claim, including a continuing claim for loss of profits of the business and interest, comes to approximately £525,000. The defendants' main ground of objection to the amount ordered to be paid into court is that the evaluation of the rebuilding cost which forms the major item in the plaintiff's claim, namely some £343,000, is on their own pleading and evidence the cost of modernisation of the major part of their premises, not simply the cost of rebuilding the demolished building. However, the judge heard this argument and in the end decided to order payment in of a sum amounting to two-thirds of the plaintiff's total claim. I cannot say, on the material before us, that he was wrong so to order.

Conclusion

I would therefore dismiss this appeal, and affirm the order made by the judge, save that:

(a) the time for compliance with the provision should be altered to enable the defendants now to comply with the condition; and
(b) there should be added a provision entitling the plaintiff to judgment for damages to be assessed if the defendants do not comply with the condition in the time required by the order.

SIMON BROWN LJ agreed and did not add anything.

Appeal dismissed. Cross-appeal dismissed. Leave to appeal to the House of Lords refused.

Copyright © Estates Gazette 2005

Appendix 1

Specimen third surveyor award

An Award under the provisions of
The Party Wall etc. Act 1996

BUILDING OWNER	Shlenter Housing Association of 29 St George Street, Mile End, London E1
BUILDING OWNER'S PROPERTY	14–16 Bishops Grove, Uxminster
ADJOINING OWNER	Mr Peregrine Hartley-Witherspoon of 12 Bishops Grove, Uxminster
ADJOINING OWNER'S PROPERTY	12 Bishops Grove, Uxminster
NOTICES	The building owner served notices on the adjoining owner on the 25 June 1999 under s 6(1) of its intention to exercise rights given to it under the Party Wall etc. Act 1996. A further notice was served on 9 July 1999 requesting the adjoining owner to appoint a surveyor in accordance with s 10.
THE SURVEYORS	The building owner has appointed George Brush, Esq, of Sam & Partners, Hartley Square, Hayes.
	The adjoining owner has appointed Anthony Blain, of 10 Dickinson Way, Harlestown, Mddx.

THE THIRD
SURVEYOR

The two surveyors not being able to agree, following notice served in accordance with s 10(8) served by Mr George Brush upon Mr Anthony Blain an application was made to the appointing officer of the Borough of Ambridge. He appointed Victor H Vegoda of Vegoda & Co Ltd, 5 Beech Avenue, Whetstone, London, N20 9JT on 18 August, 1999.

THE DIFFERENCE

The adjoining owner's surveyor has failed to declare himself incapable of acting in accordance with s 10(5) of the Act but has refused to continue to act. The two owners wish the final inspection to take place and Mr Peregrine Hartley-Witherspoon requested me to carry out a final inspection in a letter dated 6 October 2000. Accordingly I met Mr George Brush on site on 25 October 2000 to check the schedule of condition which he prepared.

FINDINGS

The schedule of condition dated 27 July 1999 was a very thorough document which correctly described the exterior and interior of the house in meticulous detail. There were only minor discrepancies due to changes made by the occupants since the schedule of condition was made.

In the kitchen there was only one cracked tile as three tiles have come away from the wall and in the small front bedroom, the cupboard has been removed.

I find that there is no discernible deterioration in the structure since the date of the schedule of condition.

It has been suggested that additional cracks not present when the schedule of condition was prepared were included in that schedule. The schedule of condition was very specific about the nature of cracks present at the time it was made. It would be a very clever trick to anticipate cracks and defects not yet present in the building and I am not persuaded that any new cracks or defects of significance have occurred since the building work commenced.

AWARD   I award that my fees for this award of £375.00 plus VAT be paid by the adjoining owner.

In witness whereof I have set my hand this 25 day of October 2000

Signature   _____

Third Surveyor   _____

Witness
Optional   _____

Appendix 2

London Building Acts (Amendment) Act 1939

PART VI.

RIGHTS &C. OF BUILDING AND ADJOINING
OWNERS.

44. In this Part of this Act unless the context otherwise Interpretation of Part VI. requires the following expressions have the meanings hereby respectively assigned to them:—

"foundation" in relation to a wall means the solid ground or artificially formed support resting on solid ground on which the wall rests;

"party wall" means —

   (i) a wall which forms part of a building and stands on lands of different owners to a greater extent than the projection of any artificially formed support on which the wall rests; and

   (ii) so much of a wall not being a wall referred to in the foregoing paragraph (i) as separates buildings belonging to different owners;

"special foundations" means foundations in which an assemblage of steel beams or rods is employed for the purpose of distributing any load.

Rights &c. of owners.

45.—(1) Where lands of different owners adjoin and are not built on at the line of junction or are built on at the line of junction only to the extent of a boundary wall (not being a party fence wall or the external wall of a building) and either owner is about to build on any part of the line of junction the following provisions shall have effect:—

Rights of
owners of
adjoining lands
where junction
line not built on

(a)   If the building owner desires to build on the line of junction a party wall or party fence wall—

    (i) the building owner shall serve notice of his desire on the adjoining owner describing the intended wall;

    (ii) if the adjoining owner consents in writing to the building of a party wall or party fence wall the wall shall be built half on the land of each of the two owners or in such other position as may be agreed between the two owners and the expense of building the wall shall be from time to time defrayed by the two owners in due proportion regard being had to the use made or to be made of the wall by the two owners respectively and to the cost of labour and materials prevailing at the time when that use is made by each owner respectively;

    (iii) if the adjoining owner does not consent in writing to the building of a party wall or party fence wall the building owner shall not build the wall otherwise than at his own expense and as an external wall or a fence wall as the case may be placed wholly on his own land;

(b)   If the building owner desires to build on the line of junction a wall placed wholly on his own land he shall serve notice of his desire on the adjoining owner describing the intended wall;

(c)   Where in either of the cases described in paragraphs (a) and (b) of this subsection the building owner builds a wall on his own land he shall have a right at his own expense at any time after the expiration of one month but not exceeding six months from the service of the notice to place on land of the adjoining owner below the level of such land any projecting footings and foundation making compensation to the adjoining owner or the adjoining occupier or both of them for any damage occasioned thereby the amount of the compensation in the event of difference to be determined in the manner provided in this Part of this Act.

(2) Nothing in this section shall authorise the building owner to place special foundations on land of the adjoining owner without his previous consent in writing.

46.—(1) Where lands of different owners adjoining and at the line of junction the said lands are built on or a boundary wall being a party fence wall or the external wall of a building has been erected the building owner shall have the following rights:—

    (*a*)   A right to make good underpin thicken or repair or demolish and rebuild a party structure or party fence wall in any case where such work is necessary on account of defect or want of repair of the party structure or party fence wall;

    (*b*)   A right to demolish a timber or other partition which separates buildings belonging to different owners but is not in conformity with the London Building Acts or any byelaws made in pursuance of those Acts and to build instead a party wall in conformity therewith;

    (*c*)   A right in relation to a building having rooms or storeys belonging to different owners intermixed to demolish such of those rooms or storeys or any part thereof as are not in conformity with the London Building Acts or any byelaws made in pursuance of those Acts and to rebuild them in conformity therewith;

(*d*) A right (where buildings are connected by arches or structures over public ways or over passages belonging to other persons) to demolish such of those buildings arches or structures or such parts thereof as are not in conformity with the London Building Acts or any byelaws made in pursuance of those Acts to rebuild them in conformity therewith;

(*e*) A right to underpin thicken or raise any party structure or party fence wall permitted by this Act to be underpinned thickened or raised or any external wall built against such a party structure or party fence wall subject to-

(i) making good all damage occasioned thereby to the adjoining premises or to the internal finishings and decorations thereof; and

(ii) carrying up to such height and in such materials as may be agreed between the building owner and the adjoining owner or in the event of difference determined in the manner provided in this Part of this Act all flues and chimney stacks belonging to the adjoining owner on or against the party structure or external wall;

(*f*) A right to demolish a party structure which is of insufficient strength or height for the purposes of any intended building of the building owner and to rebuild it of sufficient strength or height for the said purposes subject to—

(i) making good all damage occasioned thereby to the adjoining premises or to the internal finishings and decorations thereof; and

(ii) carrying up to such height and in such materials as may be agreed between the building owner and the adjoining owner or in the event of difference determined in the manner provided in this Part of this Act all flues and chimney stacks belonging to the adjoining owner on or against the party structure or external wall;

(g) A right to cut into a party structure subject to making good all damage occasioned thereby to the adjoining premises or to the internal finishings and decorations thereof;

(h) A right to cut away any footing or any projecting chimney breast jamb or flue or other projection on or over the land of the building owner from a party wall party fence wall external wall or boundary wall in order to erect raise or underpin an external wall against such party wall party fence wall external wall or boundary wall or for any other purpose subject to making good all damage occasioned thereby to the adjoining premises or to the internal finishings and decorations thereof;

(i) A right to cut away or demolish such parts of any wall or building of an adjoining owner overhanging the land of the building owner as may be necessary to enable a vertical wall to be erected against that wall or building subject to making good any damage occasioned thereby to the wall or building or to the internal finishings and decorations of the adjoining premises;

(j) A right to execute any other necessary works incidental to the connection of a party structure with the premises adjoining it;

(k) A right to raise a party fence wall to raise and use as a party wall a party fence wall or to demolish a party fence wall and rebuild it as a party fence wall or as a party wall.

(2) For the purposes of this section a building or structure which was erected before the commencement of this Act shall be deemed to be in conformity with the London Building Acts and any byelaws made in pursuance of those Acts if it is in conformity with the Acts and any byelaws made in pursuance of the Acts which regulated buildings or structures in London at the date at which it was erected.

(3) Nothing in this section shall authorise the building owner to place special foundations on land of the adjoining owner without his previous consent in writing.

47.—(1) Before exercising any right conferred on him by section 46 (Rights of owners of adjoining lands where junction line built on) of this Act a building owner shall serve on the adjoining owner notice in writing (in this Act referred to as a "party structure notice") stating the nature and particulars of the proposed work the time at which it will be begun and those particulars shall where the building owner proposes to construct special foundations include plans sections and details of construction of the special foundations with reasonable particulars of the loads to be carried thereby.

(2) A party structure notice shall be served—

    (*a*) in respect of a party fence wall or special foundations at least one month; and

    (*b*) in respect of a party structure at least two months;

before the date stated therein as that on which the work is to be begun.

(3) A party structure notice shall not be effective unless the work to which the notice relates is begun within six months after the notice has been served and is prosecuted with due diligence.

(4) Nothing in this section shall prevent a building owner from exercising with the consent in writing of the adjoining owner and of the adjoining occupiers any right conferred on him by section 46 (Rights of owners of adjoining lands where junction line built on) of this Act and nothing in this section shall require him to serve any party structure notice before complying with any notice served under the provisions of Part VII (Dangerous and neglected structures) of this Act.

48.—(1) After the service of a party structure notice the adjoining owner may serve on the building owner a notice in writing (in this Part of this Act referred to as "a counter notice").

(2) A counter notice—

    (*a*) may in respect of a party fence wall or party structure require the building owner to build in or on the party fence wall or party structure as the case may be to which the notice relates such chimney copings breasts jambs or flues or such piers or recesses or other like works as may reasonably be required for the convenience of the adjoining owner;

(b)   may in respect of special foundations to which the adjoining owner consents under sub-section (3) of section 46 (rights of owners of adjoining lands where junction line built on) of this Act require them to be placed at a specified greater depth than that proposed by the building owner or to be constructed of sufficient strength to bear the load to be carried by columns of any intended building of the adjoining owner or may include both of these requirements; and

(c)   shall specify the works required by the notice to be executed and shall be accompanied by plans sections and particulars thereof.

(3) A counter notice shall be served—

(a)   in relation to special foundations within twenty-one days after the service of the party structure notice; and

(b)   in relation to any other matter within one month after the service of the party structure notice.

(4) A building owner on whom a counter notice has been served shall comply with the requirements of the counter notice unless the execution of the works required by the counter notice would be injurious to him or cause unnecessary inconvenience to him or unnecessary delay in the execution of the works pursuant to the party structure notice.

49. If an owner on whom a party structure notice or a counternotice has been served does not within fourteen days thereafter express his consent thereto in writing he shall be deemed to have dissented from the notice and a difference shall be deemed to have arisen between the parties.

Dissent from notices

50.—(1) Where a building owner—

Underpinning

(*a*) proposes to erect within ten feet from any part of a building of an adjoining owner a building or structure independent of the building of the adjoining owner and any part of the proposed building or structure will within the said ten feet extend to a lower level than the level of the bottom of the foundations of the building of the adjoining owner; or

(*b*) proposes to erect within twenty feet from any part of an independent building of an adjoining owner a building or structure any part of which will within the said twenty feet meet a plane drawn downwards in the direction of the building or structure of the building owner at an angle of forty-five degrees to the horizontal from the line formed by the intersection of the plane of the level of the bottom of the foundations of the building of the adjoining owner with the plane of the external face of the external wall of the building of the adjoining owner;

he may and if required by the adjoining owner shall subject to the provisions of this section at the expense of the building owner underpin or otherwise strengthen or safeguard the foundations of the building of the adjoining owner so far as may be necessary.

(2) In any case to which subsection (1) of this section applies the following provisions shall have effect:—

(*a*) At least one month before beginning to erect a building or structure the building owner shall serve on the adjoining owner notice in writing of his intention to do so and that notice shall state whether he proposes to underpin or otherwise strengthen or safeguard the foundations of the building of the adjoining owner;

(*b*) The said notice shall be accompanied by plans and sections showing the site of the building or structure proposed to be erected by the building owner and the depth to which he proposes to excavate;

    (*c*)   Within fourteen days after service of the said notice the adjoining owner may serve notice in writing on the building owner that he disputes the necessity of or requires as the case may be the underpinning or strengthening or the safeguarding of the foundations of his building and if the adjoining owner serves such a notice a difference shall be deemed to have arisen between the building owner and the adjoining owner;

    (*d*)   The building owner shall compensate the adjoining owner and any adjoining occupier for any inconvenience loss or damage which may result to any of them by reason of any work executed in pursuance of this section.

(3) On completion of any work executed in pursuance of this section the building owner shall if so requested by the adjoining owner supply him with particulars including plans and sections of the work.

(4) Nothing in this section shall relieve the building owner from any liability to which he would otherwise be subject for injury to the adjoining owner or any adjoining occupier by reason of work executed by him.

51.—(1) A building owner shall not exercise any right conferred on him by this Part of this Act in such manner or at such time as to cause unnecessary inconvenience to the adjoining owner or to the adjoining occupier.

Execution of works

(2) Where a building owner in exercising any right conferred on him by this Part of this Act lays open any part of the adjoining land or building he shall at his own expense make and maintain so long as may be necessary a proper hoarding shoring or fans or temporary construction for the protection of the adjoining land or building and the security of the adjoining occupier.

(3) Any works executed in pursuance of this Part of this Act shall—

    (*a*)   comply with the provisions of the London Building Acts and any byelaws made in pursuance of those Acts; and

    (*b*)   subject to the foregoing paragraph (*a*) be executed in accordance with such plans sections and particulars as may be agreed between the owners or in the event of difference determined in the manner provided in this Part of this Act and no deviation shall be made therefrom except such as may also be agreed between the parties or in the event of difference determined in manner aforesaid.

52. Where a building owner proposes to erect any building or structure or carry out any work in relation to a building or structure on land which abuts on a street or way less than twenty feet in width the following provisions shall have effect if the erection of the proposed building or structure or the carrying out of the work involves excavation to a depth of twenty feet or more below the level of the highest part of the land immediately abutting on the street:—

Notice of excavation of sites abutting on narrow streets or ways

(*a*) Notices stating the place (being a place situate at a distance not greater than two miles of such land) at and the hours during which plans and sections of so much of the proposed building structure or work as relates to the excavation may be inspected shall be exhibited in a prominent position on the land or on any existing building or on the boundary wall fence or hoarding (if any) surrounding the said land or building and in such a manner as to be readily legible from every street or way on which the land abuts;

(*b*) The notices shall be exhibited at least four weeks before any such work of excavation is begun and shall be maintained and where necessary renewed by the building owner until such work of excavation is begun;

(*c*) The plans and sections referred to in the notices shall until the work of excavation is begun be open to public inspection without payment at the place and during such reasonable hours as are stated in the notice.

Power of entry by building owner

53.—(1) A building owner his servants agents and workmen may during usual working hours enter and remain on any premises for the purpose of executing and may execute any work in pursuance of this Part of this Act and may remove any furniture or fittings or take any other action necessary for that purpose.

(2) If the premises are closed the building owner his servants agents and workmen may if accompanied by a constable or other police officer break open any fences or doors in order to enter the premises.

(3) Before entering any premises in pursuance of this section a building owner shall give to the owner and occupier of the premises—

(*a*) in case of emergency such notice of his intention to enter as may be reasonably practicable;

(*b*) in any other case fourteen days' notice of his intention to enter.

54. Nothing in this Part of this Act shall authorise any interference with any easement of light or other easement in or relating to a party wall or prejudicially affect the right of any person to preserve any right in connection with a party wall which is demolished or rebuilt and to take any necessary steps for that purpose.

Saving for easements

Differences between owners.

55. Where a difference arises or is deemed to have arisen between a building owner and an adjoining owner in respect of any matter connected with any work to which this Part of this Act relates the following provisions shall have effect:—

Settlement of differences

(*a*) Either—

(i) both parties shall concur in the appointment of one surveyor (in this section referred to as an "agreed surveyor"); or

(ii) each party shall appoint a surveyor and the two surveyors so appointed shall select a third surveyor (all of whom are in this section together referred to as "the three surveyors");

(*b*) If an agreed surveyor refuses or for ten days after a written request by either party neglects to act or if before the difference is settled he dies or becomes incapable of acting the proceedings for settling such difference shall begin de novo;

(c)   If either party to the difference refuses or for ten days after a written request by the other party neglects to appoint a surveyor under subparagraph (ii) of paragraph (a) of this section that other party may make the appointment on his behalf;

(d)   If the difference is settled a surveyor appointed under subparagraph (ii) of paragraph (a) of this section by a party to the difference dies or becomes incapable of acting the party who appointed him may appoint another surveyor in his place who shall have the same power and authority as his predecessor;

(e)   If a surveyor appointed under subparagraph (ii) of paragraph (a) of this section by a party to the difference or if a surveyor appointed under paragraph (d) of this section refuses or for ten days after a written request by either party neglects to act the surveyor of the other party may proceed ex parte and anything so done by him shall be as effectual as if he had been an agreed surveyor;

(f)   If a surveyor appointed under subparagraph (ii) of paragraph (a) of this section by a party to the difference refuses or for ten days after a written request by either party neglects to select a third surveyor under paragraph (a) or paragraph (g) of this section the superintending architect or in cases where the Council is a party to the difference the Secretary of State may on the application of either party select a third surveyor who shall have the same power and authority as if he had been selected under paragraph (a) or paragraph (g) of this section;

(g)   If a third surveyor selected under subparagraph (ii) of paragraph (a) of this section refuses or for ten days after a written request by either party or the surveyor appointed by either party neglects to act or if before the difference is settled he dies or becomes incapable of acting the other two of the three surveyors shall forthwith select another surveyor in his place who shall have the same power and authority as his predecessor;

(*h*) All appointments and selections made under this section shall be in writing;

(*i*) The agreed surveyor or as the case may be the three surveyors or any two of them shall settle by award any matter which before the commencement of any work to which a notice under this Part of this Act to relates or from time to time during the continuance of such work may be in dispute between the building owner and the adjoining owner;

(*j*) If no two of the three surveyors are in agreement the third surveyor selected in pursuance of this section shall make the award within fourteen days after he is called upon to do so;

(*k*) The award may determine the right to execute and the time and manner of executing any work and generally any other matter arising out of or incidental to the difference:

Provided that any period appointment by the award for executing any work shall not unless otherwise agreed between the building owner and the adjoining owner begin to run until after the expiration of the period prescribed by this Act for service of the notice in respect of which the difference arises or is deemed to have arisen;

(*l*) The costs incurred in making or obtaining an award under this section and the cost of reasonable supervision of carrying out any work to which the award relates shall subject to the provisions of this section be paid by such of the parties as the surveyor or surveyors making the award determine;

(*m*) The award shall be conclusive and shall not except as provided by this section be questioned in any court;

(*n*) Either of the parties to the difference may within fourteen days after the delivery of an award made under this section appeal to the county court against the award and the following provisions shall have effect:—

(i) Subject as hereafter in this paragraph provided the county court may rescind the award or modify it in such manner and make such order as to costs as it thinks fit;

(ii) If the appellant against the award on appearing before the county court is unwilling that the matter should be decided by that court and satisfies that court that he will if the matter is decided against him be liable to pay a sum (exclusive of costs) exceeding one hundred pounds and gives security approved by the county court to prosecute his appeal in the High Court and to abide the event thereof all proceedings in the county court shall be stayed and the appellant may bring an action in the High Court against the other party to the difference;

(*o*) Where an appellant against an award brings an action in the High Court in pursuance of the last preceding paragraph the following provisions shall have effect:—

(i) If the parties agree as to the facts a special case may be stated for the opinion of the court and may be dealt with in accordance with or as nearly as circumstances admit in accordance with the rules of the court;

(ii) In any other case the plaintiff in the action shall deliver to the defendant an issue whereby the matters in difference may be tried;

(iii) The issue shall be in such form as may be agreed between the parties or in case of dispute or of non-appearance of the defendant as may be settled by the court;

(iv) The action shall proceed and the issue be tried in accordance with or as nearly as circumstances admit in accordance with the rules of the court;

(v) Any costs incurred by the parties in

the county court shall be deemed to be costs incurred in the action in the High Court and be payable accordingly.

Expenses.

56.—(1) The following provisions shall apply with respect to the apportionment of expenses as between the building owner and the adjoining owner:— Expenses in respect of party structures

> (*a*) Expenses incurred in the exercise of the rights conferred by paragraph (*a*) of subsection (1) of section 46 (Rights of owners of adjoining lands where junction line built on) of this Act shall be defrayed by the building owner and the adjoining owner in due proportion regard being had to the use which the two owners respectively make or may make of the party structure or party fence wall;
>
> (*b*) Expenses incurred in the exercise of the rights conferred by paragraph (*b*) of subsection (1) of the said section together with the expenses of building any additional party structure that may be required by reason of the exercise of those rights shall be defrayed by the building owner and the adjoining owner in due proportion regard being had to the use which the two owners respectively make or may make of the party wall or party structure required for support of the respective buildings of the two owners;
>
> (*c*) Expenses incurred in the exercise of the rights conferred by paragraph (*c*) of subjection (1) of the said section shall be defrayed by the building owner and the adjoining owner in due proportion regard being had to the use which the two owners respectively make or may make of the rooms or storeys rebuilt;
>
> (*d*) Expenses incurred in the exercise of the rights conferred by paragraph (*d*) of subsection (1) of the said section shall be defrayed by the building owner and the adjoining owner in due proportion regard being had to the use which

the two owners respectively make or may make of the buildings arches or structures rebuilt;

(*e*) Expenses incurred in the exercise of rights conferred by—

(i) paragraphs (*e*) (*g*) (*h*) (*i*) and (*k*) of subsection (1) of the said section;

(ii) paragraph (*f*) of subsection (1) of the said section in so far as the expenses are not expenses incurred in the exercise of any rights conferred by other paragraphs of the said subsection and also a fair allowance in respect of the disturbance and inconvenience caused where the expenses have been incurred in the exercise of the rights conferred by the said paragraph (*f*);

shall be defrayed by the building owner.

(2) Expenses incurred in the exercise of the rights conferred by paragraph (*j*) of subsection (1) of the said section shall be defrayed in the same manner as the expenses of the work to which they are incidental.

(3) Any expenses reasonably incurred by the building owner in executing any works in pursuance of a counter notice served on him by an adjoining owner under section 48 (Counter notices) of this Act shall be defrayed by the adjoining owner.

(4) If at any time during the execution or after the completion of works carried out in the exercise of the rights conferred by paragraphs (*e*) (*f*) (*j*) or (*k*) of subsection (1) of section 46 (Rights of owners of adjoining lands where junction line built on) of this Act any use of those works or any part thereof is made by the adjoining owner additional to the use thereof made by him at the time when the works began a due proportion of the expenses incurred by the building owner in the exercise of the rights conferred by any of the said paragraphs regard being had to the additional use of the works made by the adjoining owner shall be defrayed by the adjoining owner.

(5) Where in pursuance of section 45 (Rights of owners of adjoining lands where junction line not built on) or the said section 46 of this Act consent in writing

has been given to the construction of special foundations on land of an adjoining owner then if the adjoining owner erects any building or structure and its cost is found to be increased by reason of the existence of the said foundations the owner of the building to which the said foundations belong shall on receiving an account with any necessary vouchers within two months after the completion of the work by the adjoining owner repay to the adjoining owner so much of the cost as is due to the existence of the said foundations.

(6) Where under this section expenses are to be defrayed in due proportion regard being had to the use made by an owner of a party structure party fence wall external wall or other work regard shall unless otherwise agreed between the building owner and the adjoining owner or provided in the award also be had to the cost of labour and materials prevailing at the time when that use is made.

57.—(1) An adjoining owner may by notice in writing require the building owner before he begins any work in the exercise of the rights conferred by this Part of this Act to give such security as may be agreed between the owners or in the event of dispute determined by a judge of the county court for the payment of all such expenses costs and compensation in respect of the work as may be payable by the building owner.

Security for expenses

(2) Where in the exercise of the rights conferred by this Part of this Act an adjoining owner requires a building owner to carry out any work the expenses of which are to be defrayed in whole or in part by the adjoining owner or where the adjoining owner serves a notice on the building owner under subsection (1) of this section the building owner may before beginning the work to which the requirement or notice relates serve a notice in writing on the adjoining owner requiring him to give such security as may be agreed between the owners or in the event of dispute determined by a judge of the county court for the payment of such expenses costs and compensation in respect of the work as may be payable by him.

(3) If within one month after receiving a notice under subsection (2) of this section or in the event of dispute

after the date of the determination by the judge of the county court the adjoining owner does not comply therewith the requirement or notice by him to which the building owner's notice under that subsection relates shall cease to have effect.

58.—(1) Within two months after the completion of any work executed by a building owner of which the expenses are to be wholly or partially defrayed by an adjoining owner in accordance with section 56 (Expenses in respect of party structures) of this Act the building owner shall deliver to the adjoining owner an account in writing showing—

Account of
expenses

    (a) particulars and expenses of the work; and

    (b) any deductions to which the adjoining owner or any other person is entitled in respect of old materials or otherwise;

and in preparing the account the work shall be estimated and valued at fair average rates and prices according to the nature of the work the locality and the cost of labour and materials prevailing at the time when the work is executed.

(2) Within one month after delivery of the said account the adjoining owner may give notice in writing to the building owner stating any objection he may have thereto and thereupon a difference shall be deemed to have arisen between the parties.

(3) If within the said month the adjoining owner does not give notice under subsection (2) of this section he shall be deemed to have no objection to the account.

59.—(1) All expenses to be defrayed by an adjoining owner in accordance with an account delivered under section 58 (Account of expenses) of this Act shall be paid by the adjoining owner and in default may be recovered as a debt.

Recovery of
expenses

(2) Until an adjoining owner pays to the building owner such expenses as aforesaid the property in any works executed under this Part of this Act to which the expenses relate shall be vested solely in the building owner.

Appendix 3

Party Wall etc. Act 1996

CHAPTER 40

ARRANGEMENT OF SECTIONS

Construction and repair of walls on line of junction

Party Wall etc. Act 1996

1996 CHAPTER 40

An Act to make provision in respect of party walls, and excavation and construction in proximity to certain buildings or structures; and for connected purposes. [18th July 1996]

BE IT ENACTED by the Queen's most Excellent Majesty, by and with the advice and consent of the Lords Spiritual and Temporal, and Commons, in this present Parliament assembled, and by the authority of the same, as follows:—

Construction and repair of walls on line of junction

Section 1:

New building on line junction

1. (1) This section shall have effect where lands of different owners adjoin and—
   (a) are not built on at the line of junction; or
   (b) are built on at the line of junction only to the extent of a boundary wall (not being a party fence wall or the external wall of a building),
   and either owner is about to build on any part of the line of junction.
   (2) If a building owner desires to build a party wall or party fence wall on the line of junction he

shall, at least one month before he intends the building work to start, serve on any adjoining owner a notice which indicates his desire to build and describes the intended wall.

(3) If, having been served with notice described in subsection (2), an adjoining owner serves on the building owner a notice indicating his consent to the building of a party wall or party fence wall—

(a)   the wall shall be built half on the land of each of the two owners or in such other position as may be agreed between the two owners; and

(b)   the expense of building the wall shall be from time to time defrayed by the two owners in such proportion as has regard to the use made or to be made of the wall by each of them and to the cost of labour and materials prevailing at the time when that use is made by each owner respectively.

(4) If, having been served with notice described in subsection (2), an adjoining owner does not consent under this subsection to the building of a party wall or party fence wall, the building owner may only build the wall—

(a)   at his own expense; and

(b)   as an external wall or a fence wall, as the case may be, placed wholly on his own land, and consent under this subsection is consent by a notice served within the period of fourteen days beginning with the day on which the notice described in subsection (2) is served.

(5)   If the building owner desires to build on the line of junction a wall placed wholly on his own land he shall, at least one month before he intends the building work to start, serve on any adjoining owner a notice which indicates his desire to build and describes the intended wall.

(6) Where the building owner builds a wall wholly on his own land in accordance with subsection (4) or (5) he shall have the right, at any time in the period which—

(a) begins one month after the day on which the notice mentioned in the subsection concerned was served, and

(b) ends twelve months after that day,

to place below the level of the land of the adjoining owner such projecting footings and foundations as are necessary for the construction of the wall.

(7) Where the building owner builds a wall wholly on his own land in accordance with subsection (4) or (5) he shall do so at his own expense and shall compensate any adjoining owner and any adjoining occupier for any damage to his property occasioned by—

(a) the building of the wall;

(b) the placing of any footings or foundations placed in accordance with subsection (6).

(8) Where any dispute arises under this section between the building owner and any adjoining owner or occupier it is to be determined in accordance with section 10.

Section 2:

Right etc. of
party wall:
rights of owner

2. (1) This section applies where lands of different owners adjoin and at the line of junction the said lands are built on or a boundary wall, being a party fence wall or the external wall of a building,

(2) A building owner shall have the following rights—

(a) to underpin, thicken or raise a party structure, a party fence wall, or an external wall which belongs to the building owner and is built against a party structure or party fence wall;

(b) to make good, repair, or demolish and rebuild, a party structure or party fence wall in a case where such work is necessary on account of defect or want of repair of the structure or wall;

(c) to demolish a partition which separates buildings belonging to different owners but

does not conform with statutory requirements and to build instead a party wall
which does so conform;

(d) in the case of buildings connected by arches
or structures over public ways or over
passages belonging to other persons, to
demolish the whole or part of such buildings,
arches or structures which do not conform
with statutory requirements and to rebuild
them so that they do so conform;

(e) to demolish a party structure which is of insufficient strength or height for the purposes
of any intended building of the building
owner and to rebuild it of sufficient strength
or height for the said purposes (including
rebuilding to a lesser height or thickness
where the rebuilt structure is of sufficient
strength and height for the purposes of any
adjoining owner);

(f) to cut into a party structure for any purpose
(which may be or include the purpose of
inserting a damp proof course);

(g) to cut away from a party wall, party fence
wall, external wall or boundary wall any
footing or any projecting chimney breast,
jamb or flue, or other projection on or over
the land of the building owner in order to
erect, raise or underpin any such wall or for
any other purpose;

(h) to cut away or demolish parts of any wall or
building of an adjoining owner overhanging
the land of the building owner or overhanging a party wall, to the extent that it is
necessary to cut away or demolish the parts
to enable a vertical wall to be erected or
raised against the wall or building of the
adjoining owner;

(j) to cut into the wall of an adjoining owner's
building in order to insert a flashing or other
weather-proofing of a wall erected against
that wall;

(k)   to execute any other necessary works incidental to the connection of a party structure with the premises adjoining it;

(l)   to raise a party fence wall, or to raise such a wall for use as a party wall, and to demolish a party fence wall and rebuild it as a party fence wall or as a party wall;

(m)   subject to the provisions of section 11(7), to reduce, or to demolish and rebuild, a party wall or party fence wall to—

(i) a height of not less than two metres where the wall is not used by an adjoining owner to any greater extent than a boundary wall; or

(ii) a height currently enclosed upon by the building of an adjoining owner;

(n)   to expose a party wall or party structure hitherto enclosed subject to providing adequate weathering.

(3) Where work mentioned in paragraph (a) of subsection (2) is not necessary on account of defect or want of repair of the structure or wall concerned, the right falling within that paragraph is exercisable—

(a)   subject to making good all damage occasioned by the work to the adjoining premises or to their internal furnishings and decorations; and

(b)   where the work is to a party structure or external wall, subject to carrying any relevant flues and chimney stacks up to such a height and in such materials as may be agreed between the building owner and the adjoining owner concerned or, in the event of dispute, determined in accordance with section 10;

and relevant flues and chimney stacks are those which belong to an adjoining owner and either form part of or rest on or against the party structure or external wall.

(4) The right falling within subsection (2)(e) is exercisable subject to —

(a)   making good all damage occasioned by the work to the adjoining premises or to their internal furnishings and decorations; and

(b)   carrying any relevant flues and chimney stacks up to such a height and in such materials as may be agreed between the building owner and the adjoining owner concerned or, in the event of dispute, determined in accordance with section 10;

and relevant flues and chimney stacks are those which belong to an adjoining owner and either form part of or rest on or against the party structure.

(5) Any right falling within subsection (2)(f), (g) or (h) is exercisable subject to making good all damage occasioned by the work to the adjoining premises or to their internal furnishings and decorations.

(6) The right falling within subsection (2)(j) is exercisable subject to making good all damage occasioned by the work to the wall of the adjoining owner's building.

(7) The right falling within subsection (2)(m) is exercisable subject to —

(a)   reconstructing any parapet or replacing an existing parapet with another one; or

(b)   constructing a parapet where one is needed but did not exist before.

(8) For the purposes of this section a building or structure which was erected before the day on which this Act was passed shall be deemed to conform with statutory requirements if it conforms with the statutes regulating buildings or structures on the date on which it was erected.

Section 3:

Party structure notices

3.   (1) Before exercising any right conferred on him by section 2 a building owner shall serve on any adjoining owner a notice (in this Act referred to as a "party structure notice") stating —

(a)   the name and address of the building owner;

    (b)   the nature and particulars of the proposed work including, in cases where the building owner proposes to construct special foundations, plans, sections and details of construction of the special foundations together with reasonable particulars of the loads to be carried thereby; and

    (c)   the date on which the proposed work will begin.

(2) A party structure notice shall —

    (a)   be served at least two months before the date on which the proposed work will begin;

    (b)   cease to have effect if the work to which it relates —

        (i) has not begun within the period of twelve months beginning with the day on which the notice is served; and

        (ii) is not prosecuted with due diligence.

(3) Nothing in this section shall —

    (a)   prevent a building owner from exercising with the consent in writing of the adjoining owners and of the adjoining occupiers any right conferred on him by section 2; or

    (b)   require a building owner to serve any party structure notice before complying with any notice served under any statutory provisions relating to dangerous or neglected structures.

Counter notices **Section 4:**

4.   (1) An adjoining owner may, having been served with a party structure notice serve on the building owner a notice (in this Act referred to as a "counter notice") setting out —

    (a)   in respect of a party fence wall or party structure, a requirement that the building owner build in or on the wall or structure to which the notice relates such chimney copings, breasts, jambs or flues, or such piers or recesses or other like works, as may reasonably be required for the convenience of the adjoining owner;

(b)   in respect of special foundations to which the adjoining owner consents under section 7(4) below, a requirement that the special foundations —

(i) be placed at a specified greater depth than that proposed by the building owner; or

(ii) be constructed of sufficient strength to bear the load to be carried by columns of any intended building of the adjoining owner,

or both.

(2) A counter notice shall —

(a)   specify the works required by the notice to be executed and shall be accompanied by plans, sections and particulars of such works; and

(b)   be served within the period of one month beginning with the day on which the party structure notice is served.

(3) A building owner on whom a counter notice has been served shall comply with the requirements of the counter notice unless the execution of the works required by the counter notice would —

(a)   be injurious to him;

(b)   cause unnecessary inconvenience to him; or

(c)   cause unnecessary delay in the execution of the works pursuant to the party structure notice.

Section 5:

5.   If an owner on whom a party structure notice or a counter notice has been served does not serve a notice indicating his consent to it within the period of fourteen days beginning with the day on which the party structure notice or counter notice was served, he shall be deemed to have dissented from the notice and a dispute shall be deemed to have arisen between the parties.

Disputes arising under sections 3 and 4

Section 6:

6.   (1) This section applies where —

Adjacent excavation and construction

(a) a building owner proposes to excavate, or excavate for and erect a building or structure, within a distance of three metres measured horizontally from any part of a building or structure of an adjoining owner; and

(b) any part of the proposed excavation, building or structure will within those three metres extend to a lower level than the level of the bottom of the foundations of the building or structure of the adjoining owner.

(2) This section also applies where —

(a) a building owner proposes to excavate, or excavate for and erect a building or structure, within a distance of six metres measured horizontally from any part of a building or structure of an adjoining owner; and

(b) any part of the proposed excavation, building or structure will within those six metres meet a plane drawn downwards in the direction of the excavation, building or structure of the building owner at an angle of forty-five degrees to the horizontal from the line formed by the intersection of the plane of the level of the bottom of the foundations of the building or structure of the adjoining owner with the plane of the external face of the external wall of the building or structure of the adjoining owner.

(3) The building owner may, and if required by the adjoining owner shall, at his own expense underpin or otherwise strengthen or safeguard the foundations of the building or structure of the adjoining owner so far as may be necessary.

(4) Where the buildings or structures of different owners are within the respective distances mentioned in subsections (1) and (2) the owners of those buildings or structures shall be deemed to be adjoining owners for the purposes of this section.

(5) In any case where this section applies the building owner shall, at least one month before

beginning to excavate, or excavate for and erect a building or structure, serve on the adjoining owner a notice indicating his proposals and stating whether he proposes to underpin or otherwise strengthen or safeguard the foundations of the building or structure of the adjoining owner.

(6) The notice referred to in subsection (5) shall be accompanied by plans and sections showing —

(a)   the site and depth of any excavation the building owner proposes to make;

(b)   if he proposes to erect a building or structure, its site

(7) If an owner on whom a notice referred to in subsection (5) has been served does not serve a notice indicating his consent to it within the period of fourteen days beginning with the day on which the notice referred to in subsection (5) was served, he shall be deemed to have dissented from the notice and a dispute shall be deemed to have arisen between the parties.

(8) The notice referred to in subsection (5) shall cease to have effect if the work to which the notice relates —

(a)   has not begun within the period of twelve months beginning with the day on which the notice was served; and

(b)   is not prosecuted with due diligence.

(9) On completion of any work executed in pursuance of this section the building owner shall if so requested by the adjoining owner supply him with particulars including plans and sections of the work.

(10) Nothing in this section shall relieve the building owner from any liability to which he would otherwise be subject for injury to any adjoining owner or any adjoining occupier by reason of work executed by him.

Section 7: Rights etc.

Compensation etc.

7.   (1) A building owner shall not exercise any right conferred on him by this Act in such a manner or

at such time as to cause unnecessary inconvenience to any adjoining owner or to any adjoining occupier.

(2) The building owner shall compensate any adjoining owner and any adjoining occupier for any loss or damage which may result to any of them by reason of any work executed in pursuance of this Act.

(3) Where a building owner in exercising any right conferred on him by this Act lays open any part of the adjoining land or building he shall at his own expense make and maintain so long as may be necessary a proper hoarding, shoring or fans or temporary construction for the protection of the adjoining land or building and the security of any adjoining occupier.

(4) Nothing in this Act shall authorise the building owner to place special foundations on land of an adjoining owner without his previous consent in writing.

(5) Any works executed in pursuance of this Act shall —

(a) comply with the provisions of statutory requirements; and

(b) be executed in accordance with such plans, sections and particulars as may be agreed between the owners or in the event of dispute determined in accordance with section 10;

and no deviation shall be made from those plans, sections and particulars except such as may be agreed between the owners (or surveyors acting on their behalf) or in the event of dispute determined in accordance with section 10.

Rights of entry **Section 8:**

8. (1) A building owner, his servants, agents and workmen may during usual working hours enter and remain on any land or premises for the purpose of executing any work in pursuance of this Act and may remove any furniture or fittings

or take any other action necessary for that purpose.

(2) If the premises are closed, the building owner, his agents and workmen may, if accompanied by a constable or other police officer, break open any fences or doors in order to enter the premises.

(3) No land or premises may be entered by any person under subsection (1) unless the building owner serves on the owner and the occupier of the land or premises —

(a) in case of emergency, such notice of the intention to enter as may be reasonably practicable;

(b) in any other case, such notice of the intention to enter as complies with subsection (4).

(4) Notice complies with this subsection if it is served in a period of not less than fourteen days ending with the day of the proposed entry.

(5) A surveyor appointed or selected under section 10 may during usual working hours enter and remain on any land or premises for the purpose of carrying out the object for which he is appointed or selected.

(6) No land or premises may be entered by a surveyor under subsection (5) unless the building owner who is a party to the dispute concerned serves on the owner and the occupier of the land or premises —

(a) in case of emergency, such notice of the intention to enter as may be reasonably practicable;

(b) in any other case, such notice of the intention to enter as complies with subsection (4).

Section 9:

9. Nothing in this Act shall —

(a) authorise any interference with an easement of light or other easements in or relating to a party wall; or

(b) prejudicially affect any right of any person to preserve or restore any right or other thing

in or connected with a party wall in case of
the party wall being pulled down or rebuilt.

Section 10:

10.　(1) Where a dispute arises or is deemed to have
arisen between a building owner and an adjoining
owner in respect of any matter connected with
any work to which this Act relates either —

(a)　both parties shall concur in the appointment
of one surveyor (in this section referred to as
an "agreed surveyor"); or

(b)　each party shall appoint a surveyor and the
two surveyors so appointed shall forthwith
select a third surveyor (all of whom are in this
section referred to as "the three surveyors").

(2) All appointments and selections made under
this section shall be in writing and shall not be
rescinded by either party.

(3) If an agreed surveyor —

(a)　refuses to act;

(b)　neglects to act for a period of ten days
beginning with the day on which either
party serves a request on him;

(c)　dies before the dispute is settled; or

(d)　becomes or deems himself incapable of
acting,

the proceedings for settling such dispute shall
begin *de novo*.

(4) If either party to the dispute —

(a)　refuses to appoint a surveyor under subsection (l)(b), or

(b)　neglects to appoint a surveyor under
subsection (l)(b) for a period of ten days
beginning with the day on which the other
party serves a request on him,

the other party may make the appointment on his
behalf.

(5) If, before the dispute is settled, a surveyor
appointed under paragraph (b) of subsection (1)
by a party to the dispute dies, or becomes or
deems himself incapable of acting, the party who

appointed him may appoint another surveyor in his place with the same power and authority.

(6) If a surveyor —

(a) appointed under paragraph (b) of subsection (1) by a party to the dispute; or

(b) appointed under subsection (4) or (5),

refuses to act effectively, the surveyor of the other party may proceed to act ex parte and anything so done by him shall be as effectual as if he had been an agreed surveyor.

(7) If a surveyor —

(a) appointed under paragraph (b) of subsection (1) by a party to the dispute; or

(b) appointed under subsection (4) or (5),

neglects to act effectively for a period of ten days beginning with the day on which either party or the surveyor of the other party serves a request on him, the surveyor of the other party may proceed to act *ex parte* in respect of the subject matter of the request and anything so done by him shall be as effectual as if he had been an agreed surveyor.

(8) If either surveyor appointed under subsection (1)(b) by a party to the dispute refuses to select a third surveyor under subsection (1) or (9), or neglects to do so for a period of ten days beginning with the day on which the other surveyor serves a request on him —

(a) the appointing officer; or

(b) in cases where the relevant appointing officer or his employer is a party to the dispute, the Secretary of State,

may on the application of either surveyor select a third surveyor who shall have the same power and authority as if he had been selected under subsection (1) or subsection (9).

(9) If a third surveyor selected under subsection (1)(b) —

(a) refuses to act;

(b) neglects to act for a period of ten days beginning with the day on which either party or the surveyor appointed by either party serves a request on him; or

(c) dies, or becomes or deems himself incapable of acting, before the dispute is settled,

the other two of the three surveyors shall forthwith select another surveyor in his place with the same power and authority.

(10) The agreed surveyor or as the case may be the three surveyors or any two of them shall settle by award any matter—

(a) which is connected with any work to which this Act relates, and

(b) which is in dispute between the building owner and the adjoining owner.

(11) Either of the parties or either of the surveyors appointed by the parties may call upon the third surveyor selected in pursuance of this section to determine the disputed matters and he shall make the necessary award.

(12) An award may determine—

(a) the right to execute any work;

(b) the time and manner of executing any work; and

(c) any other matter arising out of or incidental to the dispute including the costs of making the award;

but any period appointed by the award for executing any work shall not unless otherwise agreed between the building owner and the adjoining owner begin to run until after the expiration of the period prescribed by this Act for service of the notice in respect of which the dispute arises or is deemed to have arisen.

(13) The reasonable costs incurred in—

(a) making or obtaining an award under this section;

(b) reasonable inspections of work to which the award relates; and

(c) any other matter arising out of the dispute, shall be paid by such of the parties as the surveyor or surveyors making the award determine.

(14) Where the surveyors appointed by the parties make an award the surveyors shall serve it forthwith on the parties.

(15) Where an award is made by the third surveyor—-

(a) he shall, after payment of the costs of the award, serve it forthwith on the parties or their appointed surveyors; and

(b) if it is served on their appointed surveyors, they shall serve it forthwith on the parties.

(16) The award shall be conclusive and shall not except as provided by this section be questioned in any court.

(17) Either of the parties to the dispute may, within the period of fourteen days beginning with the day on which an award made under this section is served on him, appeal to the county court against the award and the county court may—

(a) rescind the award or modify it in such manner as the court thinks fit; and

(b) make such order as to costs as the court thinks fit.

Section 11: Expenses

11. (1) Except as provided under this section Expenses expenses of work under this Act shall be defrayed by the building owner.

(2) Any dispute as to responsibility for expenses shall be settled as provided in section 10.

(3) An expense mentioned in section 1(3)(b) shall be defrayed as there mentioned.

(4) Where work is carried out in exercise of the right mentioned in section 2(2)(a), and the work is necessary on account of defect or want of repair of the structure or wall concerned, the expenses shall be defrayed by the building owner and the adjoining owner in such proportion as has regard to—

(a) the use which the owners respectively make or may make of the structure or wall concerned; and

(b) responsibility for the defect or want of repair concerned, if more than one owner makes use of the structure or wall concerned.

(5) Where work is carried out in exercise of the right mentioned in section 2(2)(b) the expenses shall be defrayed by the building owner and the adjoining owner in such proportion as has regard to—

(a) the use which the owners respectively make or may make of the structure or wall concerned; and

(b) responsibility for the defect or want of repair concerned, if more than one owner makes use of the structure or wall concerned.

(6) Where the adjoining premises are laid open in exercise of the right mentioned in section 2(2)(e) a fair allowance in respect of disturbance and inconvenience shall be paid by the building owner to the adjoining owner or occupier.

(7) Where a building owner proposes to reduce the height of a party wall or party fence wall under section 2(2)(m) the adjoining owner may serve a counter notice under section 4 requiring the building owner to maintain the existing height of the wall, and in such case the adjoining owner shall pay to the building owner a due proportion of the cost of the wall so far as it exceeds—

(a) two metres in height; or

(b) the height currently enclosed upon by the building of the adjoining owner.

(8) Where the building owner is required to make good damage under this Act the adjoining owner has a right to require that the expenses of such making good be determined in accordance with section 10 and paid to him in lieu of the carrying out of work to make the damage good.

(9) Where—

(a) works are carried out, and

(b) some of the works are carried out at the request of the adjoining owner or in pursuance of a requirement made by him, he shall defray the expenses of carrying out the works requested or required by him.

(10) Where —

(a)   consent in writing has been given to the construction of special foundations on land of an adjoining owner; and

(b)   the adjoining owner erects any building or structure and its cost is found to be increased by reason of the existence of the said foundations,

the owner of the building to which the said foundations belong shall, on receiving an account with any necessary invoices and other supporting documents within the period of two months beginning with the day of the completion of the work by the adjoining owner, repay to the adjoining owner so much of the cost as is due to the existence of the said foundations.

(11) Where use is subsequently made by the adjoining owner of work carried out solely at the expense of the building owner the adjoining owner shall pay a due proportion of the expenses incurred by the building owner in carrying out that work; and for this purpose he shall be taken to have incurred expenses calculated by reference to what the cost of the work would be if it were carried out at the time when that subsequent use is made.

Section 12:

12   (1) An adjoining owner may serve a notice requiring the building owner before he begins any work in the exercise of the rights conferred by this Act to give such security as may be agreed between the owners or in the event of dispute determined in accordance with section 10.

(2) Where —

(a)   in the exercise of the rights conferred by this Act an adjoining owner requires the building owner to carry out any work the expenses of which are to be defrayed in whole or in part by the adjoining owner; or

(b) an adjoining owner serves a notice on the building owner under subsection (1),

the building owner may before beginning the work to which the requirement or notice relates serve a notice on the adjoining owner requiring him to give such security as may be agreed between the owners or in the event of dispute determined in accordance with section 10.

(3) If within the period of one month beginning with —

(a) the day on which a notice is served under subsection (2); or

(b) in the event of dispute, the date of the determination by the surveyor or surveyors,

the adjoining owner does not comply with the notice or the determination, the requirement or notice by him to which the building owner's notice under that subsection relates shall cease to have effect.

Account for work carried out

Section 13:

13 (1) Within the period of two months beginning with the day of the completion of any work executed by a building owner of which the expenses are to be wholly or partially defrayed by an adjoining owner in accordance with section 11 the building owner shall serve on the adjoining owner an account in writing showing —

(a) particulars and expenses of the work; and

(b) any deductions to which the adjoining owner or any other person is entitled in respect of old materials or otherwise;

and in preparing the account the work shall be estimated and valued at fair average rates and prices according to the nature of the work, the locality and the cost of labour and materials prevailing at the time when the work is executed.

(2) Within the period of one month beginning with the day of service of the said account the adjoining owner may serve on the building owner a notice stating any objection he may have

thereto and thereupon a dispute shall be deemed to have arisen between the parties.

(3) If within that period of one month the adjoining owner does not serve notice under subsection (2) he shall be deemed to have no objection to the account.

Section 14:

Settlement of account

14   (1) All expenses to be defrayed by an adjoining owner in accordance with an account served under section 13 shall be paid by the adjoining owner.

(2)   Until an adjoining owner pays to the building owner such expenses as aforesaid the property in any works executed under this Act to which the expenses relate shall be vested solely in the building owner.

Section 15: Miscellaneous

Service of notices etc.

15   (1) A notice or other document required or authorised to be served under this Act may be served on a person —

(a)   by delivering it to him in person;

(b)   by sending it by post to him at his usual or last-known residence or place of business in the United Kingdom; or

(c)   in the case of a body corporate, by delivering it to the secretary or clerk of the body corporate at its registered or principal office or sending it by post to the secretary or clerk of that body corporate at that office.

(2) In the case of a notice or other document required or authorised to be served under this Act on a person as owner of premises, it may alternatively be served by —

(a)   addressing it "the owner" of the premises (naming them), and

(b)   delivering it to a person on the premises or, if no person to whom it can be delivered is found there, fixing it to a conspicuous part of the premises.

Offences

Section 16:

16 (1) If —
   (a) an occupier of land or premises refuses to permit a person to do anything which he is entitled to do with regard to the land or premises under section 8(1) or (5); and
   (b) the occupier knows or has reasonable cause to believe that the person is so entitled,
   the occupier is guilty of an offence.

   (2) If —
   (a) a person hinders or obstructs a person in attempting to do anything which he is entitled to do with regard to land or premises under section 8(1) or (5); and
   (b) the first-mentioned person knows or has reasonable cause to believe that the other person is so entitled,
   the first-mentioned person is guilty of an offence.

   (3) A person guilty of an offence under sub-section (1) or (2) is liable on summary conviction to a fine of an amount not exceeding level 3 on the standard scale.

Recovery of sums

Section 17:

17 Any sum payable in pursuance of this Act (otherwise than by way of fine) shall be recoverable summarily as a civil debt.

Exceptions in the case of Temples etc.

Section 18:

18 (1) This Act shall not apply to land which is situated in inner London and in which there is an interest belonging to—
   (a) the Honourable Society of the Inner Temple,
   (b) the Honourable Society of the Middle Temple,
   (c) the Honourable Society of Lincoln's Inn, or
   (d) the Honourable Society of Gray's Inn.

   (2) The reference in subsection (1) to inner London is to Greater London other than the outer London boroughs.

Section 19:

19 (1) This Act shall apply to land in which there is—

(a) an interest belonging to Her Majesty in right of the Crown,

(b) an interest belonging to a government department, or

(c) an interest held in trust for Her Majesty for the purposes of any such department.

(2) This Act shall apply to —

(a) land which is vested in, but not occupied by, Her Majesty in right of the Duchy of Lancaster;

(b) land which is vested in, but not occupied by, the possessor for the time being of the Duchy of Cornwall.

Section 20:

20 In this Act, unless the context otherwise requires, the following expressions have the meanings hereby respectively assigned to them —

"adjoining owner" and "adjoining occupier" respectively mean any owner and any occupier of land, buildings, storeys or rooms adjoining those of the building owner and for the purposes only of section 6 within the distances specified in that section;

"appointing officer" means the person appointed under this Act by the local authority to make such appointments as are required under section 10(8);

"building owner" means an owner of land who is desirous of exercising rights under this Act;

"foundation", in relation to a wall, means the solid ground or artificially formed support resting on solid ground on which the wall rests;

"owner" includes —

(a) a person in receipt of, or entitled to receive, the or part of the rents or profits of land;

(b) a person in possession of land, otherwise than as a mortgagee or as a tenant from year to year or for a lesser term or as a tenant at will;

(c)   a purchaser of an interest in land under a contract for purchase or under an agreement for a lease, otherwise than under an agreement for a tenancy from year to year or for a lesser term;

"party fence wall" means a wall (not being part of a building) which stands on lands of different owners and is used or constructed to be used for separating such adjoining lands, but does not include a wall constructed on the land of one owner the artificially formed support of which projects into the land of another owner;

"party structure" means a party wall and also a floor partition or other structure separating buildings or parts of buildings approached solely by separate staircases or separate entrances;

"party wall" means —

(a)   a wall which forms part of a building and stands on lands of different owners to a greater extent than the projection of any artificially formed support on which the wall rests; and

(b)   so much of a wall not being a wall referred to in paragraph (a) above as separates buildings belonging to different owners;

"special foundations" means foundations in which an assemblage of beams or rods is employed for the purpose of distributing any load; and

"surveyor" means any person not being a party to the matter appointed or selected under section 10 to determine disputes in accordance with the procedures set out in this Act.

Section 21:

Other statutory provisions

21   (1) The Secretary of State may by order amend or repeal any provision of a private or local Act passed before or in the same session as this Act, if it appears to him necessary or expedient to do so in consequence of this Act.

(2) An order under subsection (1) may —

(a) contain such savings or transitional provisions as the Secretary of State thinks fit;

(b) make different provision for different purposes.

(3) The power to make an order under subsection (1) shall be exercisable by statutory instrument subject to annulment in pursuance of a resolution of either House of Parliament.

Section 22: General

Short title, commencement and extent

22 (1) This Act may be cited as the Party Wall etc. Act 1996.

(2) This Act shall come into force in accordance with provision made by the Secretary of State by order made by statutory instrument.

(3) An order under subsection (2) may —

(a) contain such savings or transitional provisions as the Secretary of State thinks fit;

(b) make different provision for different purposes.

(4) This Act extends to England and Wales only.

Reproduced by kind permission of HMSO
Crown Copyright 1996 ©

Index